D0867815

SPOILER ALERT: YOU'RE GONNA DIE

BY KORTTANY FINN
& JACQUIE PURCELL

booktrope

Booktrope Editions
Seattle, WA 2015

COPYRIGHT 2015 KORTTANY FINN & JACQUIE PURCELL

This work is licensed under a Creative Commons Attribution-Noncommercial-No Derivative
Works 3.0 Unported License.

Attribution — You must attribute the work in the manner specified by the author or licensor (but not in
any way that suggests that they endorse you or your use of the work).

Noncommercial — You may not use this work for commercial purposes.

No Derivative Works — You may not alter, transform, or build upon this work.

**Inquiries about additional permissions
should be directed to:** info@booktrope.com

Cover Design by Greg Simanson

PRINT ISBN 978-1-5137-0462-3
EPUB ISBN 978-1-5137-0512-5
Library of Congress Control Number: 2015919035

CONTENTS

This book is first and foremost dedicated to the families that have guided my career through the past 20 years. Thank you. I'd also like to give sincere appreciation to Steve O'Brien, the best funeral director and embalmer I have ever known. It is a true honor to be able to say that I trained with you. I am forever in your debt. Thank you, SOB!

—JACQUIE

To my husband, whose love and support never wavers. And, to all of those who pushed me to write. Thank you.

—KORTTANY

And finally, to those who put their carts away, use paper plates and occasionally enjoy chili cheese fries.

—BOTH OF US

PREFACE

I have this friend named Jacquie. She lives in Yorkville, Illinois, is a wife, mom of four, and really knows how to tell a story. She also handles dead people for a living. We met in a random corner of the Internet on a forum for parents. With a few key strokes and a click she informed us that she is a deputy coroner and invited 75,000 Internet strangers, me being one of them, to "ask her anything." I don't think she expected her invitation to explode like it did, but questions poured in by the hundreds. Like most, I started reading the thread out of morbid curiosity. A person who spends her work day touching dead people is going to answer any and every question I come up with? Sign me up! Upon reading the first line of the thread, I was hooked. (Yeah. It was *that* good.) I honestly have no idea how my kids survived, considering I basically blacked out for an entire 72 hours. About halfway through this binge reading, my husband came home from work, pried the iPhone out of my hands and begged me to *at least* shower. I released my inner Gollum on him, snatched the phone back and retreated to a dark room to resume.

Aside from discovering that I clearly have some obsessive issues to work out, I made some realizations: Death is real. It's happening now. It's imminent. People all around us have died, are dying or will die. Death is something we all know is coming, yet isn't typically embraced. Death inevitably leaves loose ends. Unfortunately, due to our negligence, the people closest to us, likely consumed by the sorrow of our fresh absence, are forced to tie up these ends purely based on what they think our wishes would be. I started to understand that our society is interested in, even obsessed with, death. There are entire movies made, shows taped, and books written about it. Yet when it comes to facing the reality of our own passing we push the thoughts away or never even think them at all.

This book was birthed from Jacquie's boldness, expertise, and amazing wit. It's our hope that your thirst for all the morbid details about the life of a coroner is quenched, the subject of death becomes easier to discuss with family and friends, and that you embark on the journey of preparing your final wishes.

THE JOB

LIKE MOST PEOPLE, I don't know a whole lot about what a coroner does, (besides, you know, the whole digging around in dead bodies part.) Most of us on the parenting forum were surprised to discover just how much work goes in to the aftermath of someone's death. But aside from dealing with a death, a lot of Jacquie's days are spent in the office doing regular office tasks. As a deputy coroner, she answers phone calls, sends and receives emails and faxes, creates schedules, and teaches classes as well as managing the everyday office demands of accounts payable and receivable, payroll, budget reports, and monthly case reports. Obviously, as soon as a call is received notifying her a death has occurred, her workload dramatically increases. She's at the center of it all and facilitates every detail surrounding a death. These tasks include, but are not limited to: evaluating the scene, transporting the body to the morgue, making identifications, notifying the family, cleaning the body, answering the family's questions and showing them the body, drawing toxicology (blood, urine, vitreous[1]), scheduling autopsies, assisting autopsies, evaluating and documenting details involving the body and death, contacting funeral homes, completing death certificates and any other tasks that need to be carried out surrounding a death.

I had always imagined a coroner to be a sort of weird old man, wearing a wrinkled lab coat, sawing on a rotting body in a cold metal room. I

---

[1] *Vitreous is a thick, slightly cloudy fluid found in the eyeball. It helps the eyeball hold its shape and is used for toxicology screenings to determine things like drug and alcohol levels.*

hadn't considered, and certainly hadn't desired, being a coroner myself. The thought of standing in a room with a corpse of any kind sends chills down my spine. Upon opening the Internet thread, I genuinely expected Jacquie to be at least a little bit (or massively) creepy. But to my surprise, this wasn't the case.

I discovered that Jacquie is, in every sense of the word, amazing. She takes her work seriously, is a quality professional, and has passion for what she does. She encounters almost every aspect of death on a daily basis and has the gift of making it all sound so normal. And that, I realized, is why she is making a difference. This stuff *needs* to be normalized. It should be perfectly acceptable to discuss death in an open, informal setting and maybe even sprinkle a little humor on top. Jacquie uses her wit and grace to prove that it is indeed possible to incorporate death into a casual conversation and she encourages all of us to do the same. So, while I briefly considered becoming a coroner due to how amazing Jacquie makes it all sound, I think I'll stick with tackling the job of respectfully raising awareness of the reality of death and opening up the conversation with my loved ones. I'd encourage you to do the same! (You do, of course, still have the option of actually becoming a coroner.) Anyway, at this point you're probably getting sick of my rambling and ready to hear from the person this book is actually about. I'll let you go ahead and get to learning all the interesting stuff about Jacquie's job.

* * *

How did you decide to become a coroner?

So, here's the deal: I graduated high school early. I started college when I was 16-years-old and graduated when I was 19-years-old. (I'm not exactly sure why I was in such a hurry, but, I used to be in a huge hurry to get everything done. Now, my main goal is to lay on the couch.) I was planning on becoming a nurse until I discovered that I had to be 21-years-old to have a nursing license. I didn't like the idea of graduating and not being able to work for a year; it just didn't make sense to me at the time. Because of this, I started looking at other majors with similar prerequisites so I wasn't "reinventing the wheel" so to speak. Mortuary Science was on the list. Upon further research I learned that the minimum age was 18. I thought to myself, "That major works. I like it. Let's do it." Hand-to-God, that's how it all went down. I called my dad at work and left a message with the secretary, "Yeah... can you get a message to my dad? Tell him I'm dropping out of nursing school and transferring my major to mortuary science..." I started out in funeral directing and soon found it wasn't all I expected it to be. During that time, I met Steve O'Brien, a Chief Deputy Coroner, who then introduced me to several different coroners. He allowed me to begin an internship with him. It was there that I realized that I had discovered my calling, so I went back to school for more education and training.

Is this what you wanted to be when you grew up?

In a way. I have always been interested in this form of work. I used to play funerals with my doll. I would go back and forth between being the grieving mother and the funeral director. My own mother wanted to have me committed.

What type of education, degree, or training do you have?

My degree is in mortuary science. I'm a nationally board certified funeral director and embalmer. St. Louis University School of Medicine has a division of forensic science. I'm currently at Level 16 of their master's program specifically geared toward Advance Death Investigations. I'm a diplomate of the American Board of Medicolegal Death Investigators (www.abmdi.org) and a certified Forensic Death Investigator through the Illinois Coroner's & Medical Examiner's Association. I've done everything from examine simple nursing home deaths all the way to doing consultant work for a member of the Presidential Special Oversight Board for the Investigation of Chemical & Biological Warfare. (Personally, I think there should be a limit as to how many words can be in one government title. Seriously, that's ridiculous.)

Are coroners and medical examiners the same thing?

No. Coroners are elected officials who do death investigations. A coroner needs to be 18 or 21-years-old, depending on the state, and simply has to be elected. Obviously, to be elected, the candidate would ideally have a background consisting of both medical and legal knowledge, but it's not an official requirement. Medical examiners (ME's) are doctors who are appointed (usually) by their county boards to run offices where they have death investigators. The medical examiners are usually forensic pathologists who make up this elite subspecialty of pathology and are amazingly knowledgeable. In my area, we contract with a forensic pathologist who comes in and does the autopsies we authorize. We (as coroners and deputy coroners) are the investigators. Both are the same idea, but a different setup. Each state has its own laws and requirements. At minimum, to become a medical examiner you must be a medical doctor or osteopath[2]. In addition, a lot of states require you to have the credentials of a forensic pathologist as well, which requires many years of schooling. A person wanting to become a forensic pathologist would need to first complete

---

[2] *Osteopathy is a form of drug-free, non-invasive manual medicine that focuses on total body health by treating and strengthening the musculoskeletal framework, which includes the joints, muscles and spine. Its aim is to positively affect the body's nervous, circulatory, and lymphatic systems.*

their undergraduate degree as well as all of the schooling to become a doctor. After that they would need four to five years of pathology specialty and another one to two years for a forensic fellowship. As I said, this is an elite group of doctors and there are only about 500 practicing forensic pathologists in the U.S. (There's a definite need for more...the work is there!)

Your official job title is "deputy coroner." How is this different from "coroner"?

As I mentioned above, a coroner is an elected position. A deputy coroner is an appointed position. In most states, once the coroner is elected, they can appoint deputy coroners who, by law, can perform all of the same duties and have equal responsibilities as the Coroner. I'm currently the only full-time deputy coroner and certified death investigator in our office.

Why is the coroner an elected position? Is it a political position?

There's a long history to it, originating in medieval England. Coroners, then referred to as "Crowners," were responsible for recording all information surrounding a death. The tradition has been carried on in that a coroner is responsible for recording and investigating deaths as well as ensuring proper care is taken of the body and property. I've found it to be a mixed blessing as an elected position. Meaning, it's great that we have the power to elect a person for this position. However, because it isn't regulated, there are a lot of unqualified people doing this work throughout the country. Thankfully, the Scientific Working Group for Medicolegal Death Investigators (SWGMDI), is working to raise and establish the standards. They recommend that all coroners and staff (who aren't board certified forensic pathologists) be certified by the American Board of Medicolegal Death Investigators by the year 2020. It's nice that we're an elected office and can make our own decisions, as opposed to the appointed offices that have a board that makes their decisions for them, often without any real working knowledge of what they do. If the standards continue to improve, this position will only get better.

Running for this position actually gets very political! Locally, this past election (2012) was particularly messy for some reason. There was an editorial, I kid you not, in the local newspaper about my receipts when I went away to a training two years prior. It seriously was all, "Jacquie had a cheese stick and some trail mix. Do we really want to fund her snacks?" Truly.

Do you have to campaign for your job or is it typically an uncontested position?

I will campaign in 2016 when I run for election. Actually, I will start campaigning in 2015 when I have to get petitions signed and run in the primary. As I said, it can get very political and is quite often a contested race. My current boss is retiring, so I'm throwing my hat in the ring. I'm truly grateful that he brought me in the office and allowed me to learn the ins and outs of running it, and I'm prepared to defend my position as the best candidate in the next election.

You should very much try to find out who your coroner is. If the coroner's race is contested, research the background and experience of both candidates (as I would advocate for all elected positions). It's important to be an informed voter. When I run, I will campaign on things like having the medical knowledge and fortitude necessary to make the decisions that keep costs within budget, but are also the right decisions no matter what the cost. It's a definite balance that, in the wrong hands, could be calamitous. Also, having a medical and legal background gives me the knowledge to make good decisions when managing various types of deaths. I'll run on making certain changes in our protocol (for things like organ and tissue donation) which is a win-win for the office and the people of the county. Those sorts of things. And yes, it definitely can be a popularity contest in some counties, but most likely you should have some sort of background or knowledge in order to run and know what you're talking about during campaigning. Especially if you have an opponent.

Are there a lot of women in your field? Is it fairly even among genders or is it male or female-dominated?

There are a lot more women coming into this field, but it's still male-dominated. If you want statistics, I've done some research (meaning approximately 5 minutes of Googling), and found that there is about a 60:40 men:women ratio in this field currently. However, the ratio of students currently enrolled in school pursuing forensic science careers leans more toward the 70:30 women:men. This suggests that forensic science is one area of STEM (Science, Technology, Engineering, and Math) careers that will soon be female dominated.

Is your work schedule crazy? It's not exactly a day time only job, right?

My work schedule isn't too bad. Here's my typical day: arrive at the office at 9:00 a.m., jump on my computer and do any office-type work that I have, go home for lunch at noon to feed myself and the kids, come back to work on any office stuff I have going, then head home at 4:30 p.m. Now, this changes in a heartbeat (bad pun) if someone dies.

In that case, dispatch sends a text message to my phone that says something like, "Charlie unit requested to 123 Main Street for Code 7, subject is 28-year-old male, advise ETA." Well, that's me, Charlie 4! I generally have about a 20-30 minute response time. Deaths always take priority, so I drop what I'm doing, find care for the kids and head to the scene. If I could get people to die only between 9 a.m. and 5 p.m., and on the main floor of the house, I would, but most people aren't receptive to my advice. I primarily get called outside of office hours. I also have every nursing home or hospice death reported to me at the time it occurs, so I get a lot of those calls in the middle of the night as well. Fortunately, I don't usually have to respond to those and can manage those types of deaths over the phone. I document a bunch of information, release the body, and have the nursing home or hospice nurse call the funeral home directly to pick up the body. Not all bodies come for autopsy and not all bodies come to the morgue.

What advice do you have for people interested in this career?

If you're interested in this career, definitely get some background in medical or criminal justice and/or mortuary science. While there are currently no nationally established requirements for the job of coroner, the group I referenced earlier, (SWGMDI), will be setting them, which will make training for the job both easier (requirements will be standardized) and harder (curriculum will be demanding). A lot of coroner's offices have internship programs. Call around and see if you can intern with one. That will help you determine if you really want to do it. There are a lot of jobs available and at this point pretty much anyone can become a deputy coroner and get on-the-job training. If you want to get in this industry, now is the time to do it.

What's the best and worst part of your job?

My favorite part is having that perfect balance of variety and consistency. I get to go in the back and do science, come up front with families and do social work, go to scenes or trainings, and work at my desk. Every day is something different. I don't get stuck in that rut a lot of people get in to with their work, because it changes so much. Yet there's enough consistency that I still feel grounded, if that makes sense.

The worst is knocking on someone's door in the middle of the night to tell them their son or daughter was killed in an accident.

Does this job make you depressed?

Never. I personally think I'm good at what I do and I'm proud that I can help a family/person through this experience. I think most people who experience some sort of tragedy in their family generally have never faced this before and they don't know what to do, what to ask, what to expect, etc. They are in shock and I try to anticipate what they are going to need and answer questions for them. I do get upset when I see or hear of families that were poorly taken care of because someone didn't take the extra time to do their job well.

Have there been any cases that led you to become more involved than what is normally expected?

Yes. I think most people in this industry encounter certain cases that pull us in deeper than the standard requirements of the job. For me, it happened in November of 2008. I received a call for a hospice death. Normally, a hospice death is a simple phone call to the hospice nurse to confirm information and then we instruct the nurse to go ahead and call the funeral home directly. I was sitting up in my bed in the early morning hours, talking to this nurse on the phone, writing down the case information in my notebook. I was going through all the standard information and as I asked about the diagnosis/cause of death the nurse explained that he'd been quadriplegic for over thirty years. I did some quick math in my head and realized he'd become quadriplegic at around 20-years-old. This piqued my curiosity so I asked her how this had happened to him. She explained that when he was 19-years-old he was in the Navy and stationed in Virginia. He and a buddy had gone out on leave for a weekend and were at a bus station waiting to return to Norfolk. While standing there in their Navy uniforms, two men robbed them. They were forced down on the ground while their watches and money were taken. For some reason, as the two sailors were on the ground, one armed robber decided to shoot this man in the back. Twice. The shots rendered him immediately quadriplegic. He was transported to the hospital and his family was told that he probably wouldn't live through the night. His parents drove straight through the night to Virginia to be by his side during his last moments. However, he defied all expectations and after several surgeries, therapies, and ongoing medical treatment, he was eventually transferred back to Illinois. He finished his recovery there and was discharged, fully quadriplegic, to live back at home with his parents.

His mother devoted her life, as did the rest of the family, to his care. He would have to be rolled, changed and bathed multiple times a day. He was on a respirator to breathe. He had a wheelchair. He had a special bed. He had a lift to help get him in and out of bed. The family's home had to be renovated to accommodate all this equipment. Anyway, that one night he was given to survive turned into 38 years of care. The man ultimately developed a case of pneumonia which led to his death. However, the pneumonia he was diagnosed with was a type that commonly occurs with quadriplegics on respirators. Therefore, his cause of death was listed as: Complications of Quadriplegia due to Remote Gunshot Wound to the Back and Neck. The manner of his death was listed as homicide. Many states have circumstances where people are charged with delayed fatals. For instance, if someone who is injured as a result of someone's drinking and driving ultimately dies from those injuries, even years down the road, the original incident is revisited and the person who was drinking and driving is charged with reckless homicide. It happens regularly.

I went back to Virginia to inform them that we had a death that was ruled as a delayed fatal homicide. I wanted them to have the opportunity to charge it if they wanted to. Their response was that they never prosecuted delayed fatals because the Commonwealth of Virginia still maintained an antiquated law commonly known as the "year-and-a-day law." This law basically states that a person can only be charged with a homicide if the victim dies within one year and one day of the initial incident. What?! I argued that with today's advancements in medical technology it's not unheard of for someone to live well over a year from trauma. I disputed with various what-if scenarios, "What if a child was terribly abused and lived for thirteen months? Are you telling me the person wouldn't be charged with the homicide for killing that child?" "What if this?" "What if that?" Essentially, the district attorney answered that while he agreed the law should be changed, they had a committee put together at one point to try to change it, and they failed. He explained that the fact is, the law was there and because of that there would be no consideration of charges for this case. So, I made about twenty-million phone calls, sent copies of medical records, sent copies of reports, met with the families, had phone conferences with anyone who would listen to me, and finally found a senator who was willing to sponsor the bill to change the law. I even asked the chief medical examiner of the commonwealth at the time to go and testify before the senate about the need for the change in the law. I asked this of her with about two hours of notice, and she did it! God bless her. Anyway, I'm happy to say that on July 1, 2009, the governor signed the bill and the law was amended. There are no longer any parameters on the length of time between an incident and the time of death as a condition for charging a homicide in Virginia. I'm so super proud of the amount of work that went into that, but ultimately give all the credit to the family of Mr. Michael Clark, who helped me with everything I needed and without fail, just as they did during his life, worked tirelessly to give honor to their son and brother.

Does anything in particular make you squeamish?

There are two things I don't like: spoiled milk and decomposing bodies. And, I swear this is true, I got called one time for a man who died while eating cereal. He'd thrown up and was decomposing with the spoiled milk all over him. That one really got to me.

Do you appreciate the way coroners are portrayed in drama TV or do they have it all wrong?

I hate, hate, hate to watch shows about death investigations on TV. When I see people doing dumb stuff on there I want to start screaming, "Hey, idiot, you're wrecking our juror pool!!!" For example, these shows make it appear as if an investigation can't be complete without DNA evidence. In most every fictitious case it seems to come down to a rogue fingerprint or a loose hair to name the perpetrator and wrap up the case. The fact of the matter is, many crimes are solved without DNA. But since these shows have become so prevalent, DNA evidence seems to be the deal breaker for real-life cases when it comes to a jury needing to make a decision. This is why it's so hard to get good convictions (think Casey Anthony[3]). These shows have developed what is truly known as the "CSI effect." They have unreal expectations and come up with so many "what-ifs" that it makes things ridiculous! It seems like people look at a case and ask, "Do we have DNA?" No. "Well, then, I don't know what else we can possibly do here. Let's add this to the 200,000+ unsolved deaths and we'll come back to it someday if technology advances." The reality is, the offender for the majority of all unsolved cases is listed in the case notes and is usually someone who'd been mentioned or interviewed within the first five days of the investigation.

DNA analysis costs a ton of money and isn't used as often as is made out to be on TV. Everyone certainly doesn't have access to the amazing equipment and technology used to investigate crimes portrayed in those shows either. So, where the general public expects DNA to be the bow on top of the nicely packaged-up case, it isn't, and this causes people to start having doubts, and doubt is a malignancy to common sense. I'm not downplaying the use of DNA here, because it's definitely used and has its place in the world of making and/or breaking cases and weeding out the innocent. It just isn't used all the time and I think that's an example of one of the misperceptions these shows create. I don't envy the prosecutors who have to work so hard on some of these cases. I remember one training I attended where I learned of a study done which essentially determined that there is no true "CSI

---

[3] Casey Anthony, a mother from Florida, was charged with the murder of her 2-year old daughter, Caley. Even though public opinion heavily favored her guilt, a jury acquitted her in 2011. Many believe the jury's decision was based on the lack of evidence establishing guilt and the prosecution's failure to meet its burden of proof beyond a reasonable doubt.

effect." However, I've seen instances where I would definitely say the juror/jury fits the profile.

Do you think your experiences on the job have shaped the way you view people and the world around you?

I remember going to my first homicide case: It was a 30-year-old man who'd been shot dead in a gang shooting. I actually said, "He's 30-years-old! He should know better than this!" Now I know I was just extremely naive back then. I've since realized that the majority of people: 1) don't have a clue what can kill them, 2) truly believe it won't happen to them, and 3) don't believe they could kill someone else by their actions (or believe they can get away with what they're doing wrong—think drinking and driving—just one more time).

I'll also say that this job has made me painfully aware of the fragility of life. I'm always cognizant that at any moment a drunk driver could crash into me on the road. Or that when I drop my kids off at school it could be the last time I see them because someone could come and start shooting at any moment. I'm aware that a random accident or a sudden illness could happen at any moment and claim the life of someone I love. I know that each minute I have here is a gift from God and I live life with this knowledge at the forefront of my mind.

Do you feel like you have increased fears about death of your children since I'm sure you see children their age that are deceased?

All the time. I once told my son he couldn't get a driver's license until he witnessed an autopsy from a car accident. He wasn't too keen on the idea and asked, "What if you just describe the autopsy and I can imagine what it was like?" I replied, "That's fine. Then you can describe where you want to drive to and I can imagine you getting there."

He still hasn't seen an autopsy, and I would never force him to come, of course. But I've done my best to make him aware of the heavy responsibility we all carry as licensed drivers. He did help me on a double fatal car accident scene. The kids were both only a couple years older than him. He certainly didn't like it and I hope the reality of what could happen resonates with him.

Would you say you go to the doctor a lot more than other people, or are you the opposite and go less because you're more knowledgeable?

This job has definitely turned me into somewhat of a hypochondriac. I've actually heard this from my doctor (with whom I have a great relationship), "Get out of my office. I have real patients to see!" Our pediatrician has said on a few occasions, "Knowledge isn't always a good thing, Jacquie, your kid is fine!"

What safety precautions have you implemented in your own life since working in this field?

There are a lot of little things: wearing helmets on bikes, skateboards, scooters, etc. I put reflector tape on all sides of my strollers. I secure large items in my vehicle to prevent them from being thrown around inside the vehicle in case I crash. I will always pull my foot off the gas, steer the wheel and coast as opposed to hitting the brake or turning the wheel quickly. (We see a lot of over-correction crashes.)

I didn't allow my son to play football because I attended a training titled "Sports-Related Head Injuries in Children." You just can't come back from some of those studies unchanged. I'm so glad they've developed a big push for guidelines to follow for children with concussions and proper training for coaches.

Have you developed any strong views or beliefs due to things you've witnessed on the job?

After seeing so many drug-related cases, I've definitely developed some opinions on drugs and their usage. For example, I would never use fentanyl for pain unless I had terminal cancer, or it was being administered in the hospital. Never on my own. It's a crazy addictive opiate drug, more powerful than heroin, and I've seen the damage it can do. Also, I would encourage people who are suicidal to talk to family members (or anyone for that matter). The family and friends left behind are so sad and often feel incredibly guilty. I really do believe that many of them would have tried to offer more help if they'd known the person was desperate enough to harm themselves.

Has your faith been impacted by this profession?

The situations I encounter at work have certainly affected my faith. I've heard, and seen, too much to dismiss a higher level to our existence. I also struggle a lot. How is a loving and merciful God allowing children to be murdered and abused to death while some terrible people live on? I have a lot of questions and opinions, but I often chalk it up to an answer that is beyond my understanding. I trust that one day I will know the answers. (Or hope I will!)

I used to stand by respectfully as priests or reverends said prayers over the bodies at scenes. Now I join in if I know the prayers. I also realize that every faith has its beliefs about what happens in the afterlife and I try to be respectful of whatever their concerns are. Personally this causes more questions within my own faith, but I leave with deeper trust that the answers are forthcoming.

Do you tend to get emotional about cases you're working or is it something you can push aside for the job?

It varies. Sometimes I become sad. Sometimes I get mad; I've yelled at bodies, especially when someone does something stupid, like overdose, and leaves their kids behind or unattended because of it. Sometimes I have to hold it all in and stay strong. For example, I once had a woman killed in a car accident. She was just out running errands. I went to her home to make notification, and the only people there were her two kids aged 13 and 10. I found out that their dad lived halfway across the country. They talked to him, but rarely saw him. The 13-year-old got him on the phone and I privately told him what had happened. He was going to hop on a plane right away.

I told him that the kids were scared and wanted to know what was happening. I asked what he wanted me to tell them. He said to tell them about the crash since they'd just moved there and there was really no one else he knew of to do it. So, I went back in, sat the kids down and very gently told them what had happened. This little 10-year-old boy jumped into my arms and was screaming, "Don't leave me, don't leave me!" (It makes me tear up just remembering this.) I told them I wasn't going to leave them and we were going to figure some things out. Then, the boy ended up getting so angry. (He seriously went through all the stages of grief right in front me.) He was shaking mad at the person who crashed into his mom.

After a few hours we contacted an aunt who lived in the area, and she was very loving and caring, so I felt comfortable enough to leave. I was very emotionally invested in that one, but I had to stay strong for the kids as well as do my job.

Are there any other professions that interest you, aside from your current one?

I would love to be a food critic in Bora Bora! But, if I wanted to keep my mind busy and do something different, I always thought being a forensic geneticist sounded like a neat thing. I'd also like to be a forensic anthropologist, but, I don't like the idea of boiling bones...it kind of creeps me out.

Say someone dies right now. You get the call. What happens next?

I let dispatch know I will be en route and give them my approximate time (usually within 30 minutes). Let's assume it's a car accident scene: I stop whatever I'm doing and go to my office where I pick up my work van. I drive to the accident location. Upon arriving at the scene, I meet with law enforcement who give me the breakdown of what happened. I then get a list of what we're still waiting for: pictures, accident reconstruction, etc. Next, I approach the decedent and evaluate the scene around them. I may take some photos or measurements for my own records as well. Then, often utilizing the help of the fire personnel on scene, the body is placed in a body bag and onto my cot. I load the cot into my van and transport the body back to my morgue.

When I get back, I often have to make notification to the family. So, I confirm the person's identification. If they live locally, I go to their home and make notification to their family. Many times, the family wants to come back to the morgue and view the body of the decedent. I have them come about 10 or 15 minutes behind me which gives me an opportunity to get back to the morgue, clean up the body and prepare them for a family viewing. Then, I meet with the family in our conference room. I answer any of their questions. I let them know what they need to do next. I try to anticipate any needs they may have and address those as needed. Then, I prepare them for what they're about to see. For example, I might say, "He's lying on a table, in a body bag, but he's draped with a sheet. You'll see his head, chest and his right arm/hand. He has several abrasions and a laceration on his forehead. He has a little bit of blood that was coming from his nose. I've stopped it now, but it may continue, especially if you move him. You can touch him, kiss, and hug him, whatever you're comfortable with." Then, I direct them into the family viewing area.

After the family has had their time, they leave and then what happens next depends on the case. In a car accident scenario, I may just draw toxicology (blood, urine, vitreous), or if someone was at fault for the car accident and the possibility of reckless homicide charges may be there, then I'll schedule an autopsy. If we decide the autopsy is necessary, the body is placed back into the cooler and toxicology is drawn at the autopsy. If no autopsy is needed, I will draw the toxicology right away and then put the body back into the cooler. After that, the body is either pending autopsy or pending release to funeral home, depending on the circumstances.

Once I get the toxicology results back, I forward those results to the doctor who uses that information in combination with the autopsy findings to finalize the cause of death. In our county, we decide the manner of death if it's obvious (natural, accident, suicide, homicide or undetermined). If the circumstances aren't clear for determining a manner of death we may hold an inquest where a panel of jurors is summoned to convene and decide on the manner of death.

With an inquest, a panel of jurors is summoned through the standard jury pool process. Usually, the lead investigator in the case is subpoenaed to give testimony as to their current findings in the investigation. The jury is given the opportunity to ask questions of the investigator. There may be other people who testify based on the circumstances of the case (e.g., witnesses, other forensic professionals, police, family members). The family sometimes is represented by legal counsel who may attend and can ask questions of the witness(es). Sometimes, the state's attorney may be present and ask questions. The coroner usually provides the jury with the autopsy and toxicology findings. The jury is simply tasked with determining the manner of death, be it natural, accident, suicide, homicide or undetermined.

The jury also has the opportunity to give recommendations. Recommendations could be something as simple as suggesting a road study in a particularly bad, dangerous or deadly section of road to see if stop signs or stop lights or additional signage may be appropriate. In the event of a homicide, blame may be placed on a person responsible and the jury can name that person. In our state, coroner's inquests are not mandatory (although they were only a few years ago) and we really don't hold coroner's inquisitions very often at all.

Obviously, each death scene is different. For example, I would do things differently for a suicidal hanging than I would for a suicidal gunshot wound. But that's the gist of it.

Can you explain more about how and why you do toxicology testing?

I'll start with the how: If I'm going to draw toxicology I will draw blood, urine and vitreous. I'll take a small (maybe 10-20cc) syringe and needle and insert the needle in the white of the eye just outside the iris (colored area). Once I see that needle pass into the pupil (a hole in the eye with a muscle ring/sphincter that opens and closes to allow light in or reduce the amount of light) then I will gently press down on the eyeball while pulling back on the plunger of the syringe. This causes the fluid to enter the syringe and the eyeball flattens. We (or the funeral home) will use an eye cap, which is a type of hard plastic contact lens that fits over the eye and returns it to its natural shape. Second, I'll take a large syringe (60cc) and needle (16 gauge – 4 inch) and insert the needle in the area above the right clavicle (collar bone) sort of in that soft area inside that bony triangle there. I'll push the needle all the way in and then slowly withdraw the needle while pulling back on the plunger and as soon as it hits the artery (usually the subclavian, but it varies) I stop withdrawing and just maintain pulling back on the plunger until I get as much blood as I need. Now, in some circumstances—if there's been a lot of blood loss at a scene due to extensive trauma—this might be very difficult. It may take several attempts and I may have to try several locations before I get enough blood to test. Finally, I'll take another large syringe and needle and insert it just above the pubic symphysis (commonly known as pubic bone) and at about a 45 degree angle downward until the needle enters the urinary bladder. I will pull back on the plunger, retrieve the urine (if there is any – usually there is some residual urine) and put it into a urine toxicology container. I then package up these samples, send them off to a commonly used forensic toxicology lab and wait for the results.

Now, to the why: The lab tests the samples for whatever we request. Usually it's alcohol and drugs of abuse which is a list of hundreds upon hundreds of illicit and prescription drugs. The test is first run for qualitative results (meaning positive and negatives) and then the positive results are rerun for quantitative results, which gives us actual levels of medications, illicit drugs, alcohol, what have you. I receive the results, and if we did an autopsy I'll forward them to the pathologist who will use the results to finalize the cause and manner of death. If we didn't do an autopsy, I will interpret the results and respond accordingly. Sometimes this means that someone is going to be charged for a crime, or just serves as knowledge that someone did or did not have something in their systems, or it simply confirms suspicions, and so forth. Most of the time we have a pretty good idea already of the results we'll receive back, but there are occasions that leave us completely shocked. (Like when known drug abusers come back with completely negative results.)

Why does vitreous get used for things like toxicology reports?

Vitreous, the fluid found in eyeballs, holds all of the same levels as you would see in the blood (alcohol and drugs) but, because it isn't constantly being filtered through the liver and kidneys, it's much more stable. We can actually compare the alcohol level of the vitreous fluid to that of the blood and build a story as to whether or not the subject has been drinking for a long time and is coming down from a higher alcohol level or just started drinking and is still building up an alcohol level. We can also assess the vitreous for electrolytes and tell if a subject was dehydrated or possibly in ketoacidosis if they are a diabetic. The vitreous fluid is actually the more ideal fluid for numbers; however, it wouldn't exactly be practical to test in living persons, so, it isn't used. Although, I suspect that if you were at risk of having your vitreous drawn and tested for alcohol levels it would deter a lot of drinking and driving!

What's the most common cause of death you see?

Natural deaths: various forms of cancer. Accidental deaths: overdoses. Suicides: hangings. Homicides: Gunshot wounds.

Are certain bodies harder to examine then others?

Does it get to me? Usually only babies and kids are tough to examine. Especially in the cases of child abuse. I always take extra special care because I think, sadly, that being in my cooler is the first peace the poor child ever "knew." I think about my work, the people who have died and their families all the time. I can't speak for everyone, obviously, but personally, I always take special care of the babies and kids. Always. I keep them wrapped in a blanket, not a body bag. And I leave the lights on for them...weird, I know, but I do.

How, as a mother, do you keep your composure when having to go tell another mother that her child is dead?

It's very tough, but props to moms, they take care of their kids to the end. Truly, it's the dads I see fall apart easier. I've seen grown men literally have to be carried in my office to come and view their child. I'm not saying moms don't grieve; they do. They crawl up on their child's body and scream and wail and cry and I very often tear up right with them. It's a primal sounding cry. I hope you never have to hear it. I also think this job has made me a better mother. I've realized, mostly as my son aged into his 15th, 16th, and 17th years, that he's not a small adult, but in fact a large child, both physically and mentally, and it's helped a lot with understanding and guiding him.

What's the craziest reaction you've gotten from someone when you told them a family member is dead? Have you had anyone get mad at you? (Displaced anger, etc.) Anyone not believe you?

Oh, people yell at me, throw things at me, try to hit me...I've been locked out on the front porch because the people are too hysterical to open the door when they realize I'm there. I try not to tell them at the door but at two in the morning when someone's knocking at your door, you read my badge and it says coroner...people put it together pretty quickly. These are rare though. Mostly people just have questions and want to know what happened. Sometimes people just want to see the body and other times people can't cope and have me talk to someone else. It varies.

A NOTE FROM JACQUIE

My job is so special to me. I hate thinking of it as a "job"—it seems to trivialize what I do. So much of my heart goes out to these families that I work with on a daily basis. I often think of it like this: if my dinner gets interrupted because I have to go on a call, so be it, I'll have the opportunity for another dinner with my family. But this family, they won't have that opportunity with their loved one again. They need me and my expertise, something absolutely no one else can offer them, and they need me right now. I've learned how to balance my life so that I'm still capable of juggling my family's needs with the needs of the people I took an oath to serve. I don't take that responsibility lightly.

DEATH

CONSIDERING THE NATURE of her job, those of us on the parenting forum basically dubbed Jacquie the "Queen of Death" and assumed she'd be able to answer all of our burning questions on the subject. While she claims she isn't omnipotent, I swear she comes about as close as one can get.

The circumstances of a person's death are oftentimes heartbreaking. However, many of us feel this strange pull to want to know all the details surrounding a person's passing. The second I hear that someone has passed away, my first questions are, "How did they die? What happened?" I'm not really sure what drives this common curiosity, but I know that hearing the details of a person's death, in addition to being incredibly fascinating, possesses a great amount of power to shape beliefs, provide awareness, and educate others. Jacquie, of course, has more than enough stories about death to go around. We begged her to share them and she didn't disappoint. (Does she ever?) Enjoy!

* * *

In your opinion, what's the worst way to die?

Being killed by someone you love.

If you got to choose, how would you want to die?

I would drive myself home after my 100th birthday celebration, where everyone came to wish me well, crawl into my very comfy bed and die peacefully in my sleep. My private caretaker would come in and find me in the morning and take care of things from there.

If you were going to commit suicide, how would you do it?

If I was going to kill myself, and I didn't care that they knew it was suicide, I would use carbon monoxide in the garage. If I wanted everyone to be stuck, unable to discover the cause of my death, I would overdose on insulin.

What do you think is the most "painless" way to die?

During surgery. But that's just my opinion. Honestly, I have no idea. My "clients" don't leave me reviews. I would have to search around like anyone else for near-death experiences and see what they thought.

Have you ever seen someone die of a broken heart?

I've been involved in several cases where older couples die within days or months of each other, sometimes even right at the anniversary date of the other spouse's death. Obviously that isn't conclusive, but I do think there's something to it.

Do you think people should be put out of their misery when there's no chance of survival?

As a general rule, no. I think this leaves too much open for lay interpretation and doesn't give people a chance, even if the possibility is slim, to get help or recover. I don't feel that it's right for someone to be able to take that away. Under certain circumstances I can see where it seems like it would be okay, but there are just too many unknowns.

Do you believe people know when it's their time to die?

Yes, I do believe many people know when it's their time to go, and that is generally very comforting to families. However, I also know there are times where sudden death is just that, sudden, and completely unexpected. It's horribly tragic for some families, even if it's a natural cause. I want to say this: You are going to die. It's amazing to me how people are so unprepared and don't talk about it ahead of time. Families are left having no idea what their loved one wanted after they pass away. I can remember going to a death scene and asking the family which funeral home they wanted me to call for removal of the body. They said, "I don't know...it was just so unexpected." I hope the look on my face didn't convey what I was shouting in my head, "Are you kidding me?! She's 93 and in a hospital bed in your dining room! How unexpected could this possibly be?!"

Just think about it: When you die, your loved ones are going to be tasked with, among many other things, knowing all of the information for your death certificate. Do they even know your mother's maiden name? Do they know exactly where you were born? Do they know your social security number? If you were in the military, do they know where to find a copy of your DD-214? Do they know whether want an open casket viewing, a direct cremation or something completely different? Our families want to spend time honoring us after our death. Respect that time and prepare as much as possible for your death so they don't have to.

Do you believe in ghosts?

I have no personal experience with ghosts. I do believe they exist, but the spirits are attached to people and places. Not coroners. Their physical bodies mean nothing to them; they hang with their people.

Seriously...you work with the dead and you really have had no paranormal experiences?

Truly, I've never had a weird thing happen that I couldn't explain. Well, there is one thing I consider odd. I'm not sure this has anything to do with my work stuff, it could just be my general "energies" (ugh, that sounds very tree-hugger and that is not me) but clocks have a hard time staying set around me. It frustrates the heck out of my husband, but we constantly have to reset the clocks. The clocks in my house, the one in my car, and at my office, too. They just constantly begin to run fast. Analog, digital, atomic, it doesn't matter, they all end up changing around me at some point.

What's the strangest cause of death you've come across?

There are so many... We found a guy down in a sewer once. He was covered in what appeared to be barnacles. I had a guy randomly die up on the roof of a house. That was a treat to investigate. The removal was even more fun. I had a little boy (age 6) stick his head out of the car window and break his neck on a tree branch. It was so sad, and a very freak accident. I had a worker hang himself from the rafters of an office supply store. Once, a guy called 911 to report a robbery, but really when the cops got there, he'd killed himself and left a note. He just wanted to be found before his son got back. I had a woman who jumped out of her truck to close the gate at the end of the driveway. She left the truck in drive and quickly tried to jump back in. The truck rolled forward and pinned her inside the door against the fence gate.

She was pinned there, just feet from the road with cars going by all day, but from the road it looked like the truck was just parked, so no one knew to help her. They're all sad and unfortunately I could go on and on...

Why is it that people are often found either undressed or partially undressed when they died?

That does happen a lot! My guess is that before people die they often either, a) don't feel well and want to lie down, so they start stripping off clothes to get comfortable, or b) feel like they need to use the bathroom and take some of their clothes off for that. A lot of heart attack victims are found in the bathroom. We call it the death poop. You DO NOT want to take this poop. If you are having symptoms of a heart attack and feel like you need to go to the bathroom, call an ambulance or rush to a hospital emergency room! Any reason aside from those is kind of a case-by-case situation.

This "death poop" you speak of is utterly horrifying. Can you elaborate on that so I don't have to fear for my life every time I need to poop?

It does sound pretty horrifying, right? What I'm getting at is that quite often the signs of cardiac disease will mimic flu-like symptoms. People mistake the pressures caused by a heart attack as the pressures of needing to urgently use the bathroom. It's not uncommon to find someone who's died from sudden cardiac-related issues on the toilet or lying on the floor of the bathroom. Rest assured that it isn't usually sudden. Symptoms of cardiac disease usually manifest for a few weeks or months before a heart attack. Educate yourself on what to look for. People will often have symptoms like pressure or burning in their chest and chalk it up to something benign like heartburn. (This is an especially common symptom in post-menopausal women.) If a person in your life has a sudden onset of heartburn for a few weeks or begins using a lot of antacids, it would be prudent to recommend they have a thorough cardiac work-up to ensure there aren't more serious problems occurring.

I might be beating a dead horse here, but I really feel I need to sort of drill this in. I don't care who you are, if you have a bottle of Tums or Rolaids on your nightstand, you need to have a cardiac work-up with your doctor immediately. As I may have mentioned before, one of the most common effects of cardiac disease is sudden death. And one of the most common signs of cardiac disease – often overlooked – is misinterpreted heartburn. (I'm currently imagining cardiologists all around scratching their heads at the sudden influx of patients knocking down their doors asking for EKGs and angiograms because they've had a bout of heartburn. I'm sure they'll forgive me when the contractor comes by to finalize the plans for their new dream home.)

The thing is, I remember distinctly telling my father during the year 1995 (which was super early in my career, but I'd seen it enough to know it was relevant and serious), in which he was constantly taking Tums, that he had heart disease. He was overweight and had a sedentary lifestyle. My mother made elaborate, tasty dinners of butter and cream with red meat. And for dessert, he had Tums. Without fail, every night. Finally, I said to him, "Dad, you have heart disease." He was 45 and pretty much dismissed me with your typical, "I'm fine" response. I nagged and nagged until he finally got frustrated and told me to knock it off. So I did. Then, I very passive-aggressively gave him a large bulk bottle of Tums for Christmas that year. Within six months he had my mother blowing through stop lights as she raced him to the hospital while he was having a heart attack. He's had six stents since then and is very lucky his blockages didn't result in a need for a CABG (coronary artery bypass graft, commonly known as heart bypass) or worse, sudden death. Fast forward 20 years and his heart is still holding up pretty well, but I know his next cardiac event will most likely require bypass, if he makes it that far.

Then, there was the situation with my mother just last year when she visited the ER on several occasions with severe heartburn and they sent her home with medicine for GERD (gastroesophageal reflux disease). It wasn't until her final trip that someone finally said, "Hmmm, she keeps ending up in the ER, she's post-menopausal, a smoker and she eats cream and butter (although her weight is fine). She seems to fit the perfect picture for the 'silent heart attack' in women that medical professionals always talk about." She had stents put in the next morning. The point I am trying to make here is that a leading cause of death is cardiac disease and it often presents differently than you'd expect. By the time it's critical, it is presenting as one would expect, with typical, textbook symptoms, and by then it's often too late. That's a shame when there's frequently so much time leading up to it to get help. Days, weeks, months of antacids, chest tightness, pain, difficulty breathing with exertion, tiredness, flu-like symptoms, congestion—all of these can be signals of impending cardiac events and when noticed in combination with other risk factors such as poor eating habits, excessive alcohol consumption, sedentary lifestyle, high stress levels, previous diagnosis of high blood pressure and/or high cholesterol, it's time to get to the doctor. Also, please note the following: high blood pressure is heart disease and high cholesterol is heart disease. I'm often told that someone doesn't have any cardiac history, but find out later that they take medicine for high blood pressure and high cholesterol. I think people don't realize that those two conditions are actually very serious.

Have you ever been unable to determine a cause of death?

Yes, there's a case I still wonder about. There was a man who committed suicide in his garage via carbon monoxide. The whole thing was recorded on audio tape so it appeared to be a very cut and dry case. I drew toxicology and released the body. For some reason I decided to take toxicology to the hospital to run a rapid CO (carbon monoxide) level. It came back 5.2. Not nearly enough CO to kill you. That's the CO level of a regular smoker. Our CO deaths come back with levels of 60, 70, 80 or 90, not 5.

I quickly called the funeral home and told them not to embalm him and that I was coming to get him. He had to have been completely dead within seconds (on the tape you hear him start the car) because even if he'd only passed out he would still be breathing and would have a higher CO level. The only possible explanation had to be that he died from something else before breathing in all that carbon monoxide. It was so odd.

We didn't find anything at his autopsy that showed a cause of death. In fact, he had an anomaly in his heart that actually made it better than most hearts in the majority of the population. There was nothing wrong with this guy. Nothing. He did have an alcohol level of .17, not much, but if you aren't a regular drinker it can be high. I think we used that to incorporate a cause of death, but I still don't really know exactly what happened to him. It was incredibly sad, the reason for his attempted suicide. He said in his note (verbal note, on tape) that he was "so sorry" and he was doing this because he got caught stealing. He was a greeter at a store and took a package of Tucks pads. He had hemorrhoids that were bothering him and he was too embarrassed to buy them.

Have any particular murder cases stood out to you?

I remember this case like it was yesterday. It was March 8, 1999, and I was called to an apartment/townhome for an 18-year-old girl who had been stabbed to death. It was, without a doubt, one of the worst scenes I've ever worked. This poor girl was home alone with her 3-year-old sibling. She had graduated high school and was taking a few college courses, but was responsible for watching her sibling on certain days of the week. On this particular day, she was home with the 3-year-old while her mom was at work and her 8-year-old sibling was at school. She was in the shower when her mother's boyfriend entered the home, went into the bathroom and attempted to make a sexual pass at her. There was a radio on the back of the toilet and she threw it at him. He went downstairs, grabbed a kitchen knife, came back and stabbed her to death. This poor girl fought so hard for her life. She was obviously wet and naked and at such a disadvantage to this man who was fully dressed, dry, and much stronger. The walls of the bathroom were red with blood. She really fought so damn hard. I cringe to think what the 3-year-old may have witnessed.

In a complete case of happenstance, the 8-year-old had fallen ill and the school called the mom to come and pick him up. Mom returned home, unexpectedly and in the middle of the day, intruding on the tail end of this fight. The boyfriend walked right out the front door and made some flippant comment to her like, "I killed her" or "she's dead." Something like that. (I've often wondered if the mother coming home at that moment had saved the life of that 3-year-old. Obviously I will never know.) The mom ran upstairs and found her beautiful daughter in the bathroom. This was back when we still had landline telephones on the walls. You could follow the mom's bloody footprints coming down the stairs and directly to the phone to call 9-1-1 then follow the bloody footprints going back up the stairs to try to tend to her daughter again. As a mother, I can't even imagine. It was a scene that was difficult for me to be involved in and I didn't even know that poor girl. After it was all said and done, I believe he was sentenced to 80 years in prison. I often wonder where her family is today and how they're doing.

Another case I think about is the double homicide of a husband and wife. I believe they ultimately found that this couple was murdered over drug money, but I'm not positive that was the official reason. The couple had two children, 4-year-old and 9-month-old boys, and lived in an apartment. The individuals who murdered the couple entered the apartment and put the 4-year-old in the back bedroom. They used a phone cord to tie up the man and woman, laid them on the floor face-down on pillows and shot each of them in the back of the head. The 9-month-old was just crawling freely around the apartment while this occurred. The 4-year-old was scared and didn't come out of his room until morning. When he did, he found his parents dead in the kitchen. The baby, covered in blood from crawling all over mom and dad all night, was just hanging out in the kitchen. The little boy went out of the apartment and knocked on the door across the hall. He told the neighbor that his mom and dad were dead. The neighbor came over, saw the scene, grabbed the two kids and called 9-1-1 right away. It was gruesome, cold-hearted and disgusting. I remember every detail of that scene. This was a case from my early days, around 1996 or 1997 and it impacted me tremendously. I often wonder what happened to those little guys. I wonder if they used that tragic experience and built a better life for themselves or if the tragedy got the best of them and they ended up misdirected. Sometimes I want to know the answer, and sometimes I don't.

Do you encounter many gang-related murders?

I've been involved in the investigation of around 40-50 gang-related homicides. Twenty or more of which were in the year 2000. It was a busy year for gangs. Gang shootings are sad in the sense that they're almost exclusively young men (aged 15-25) who had such rough upbringings that joining a gang seemed like the lesser of evils when it came to the options of what to do with their lives. However, I'm also well-aware there are a number of kids who are brought up in unstable homes and go on to choose healthy and productive paths. I don't think it's the default lifestyle for anyone in an unstable situation.

Anyway, I have investigated many gang shootings, but several stick out in my mind. The first one is the case of Little Nico. He'd just turned 6-years-old and was spending the night at his grandparent's house in preparation for a birthday celebration the next day. Unfortunately, he went to sleep in his uncle's bed. His uncle was an older teen at the time and involved in a gang. He was the intended target when a member of a rival gang shot through his bedroom window that night and shot little Nico several times in the back. A completely happy, innocent little boy curled up sleeping in bed and his life ended with a couple of blind shots to his back. Disgusting and sad all at once.

There was the time a young man, 16 years of age, was shot in a gang shooting with an AK-47. That's right; these teens are shooting each other with AK-47s! I remember being at the hospital and taking the boy's mom in a separate room to let her know that her son had died. She was bawling crying. She started to explain that her son had been living at his older brother's house, but that he was getting into too much trouble so she had recently brought him home. She felt like she was finally getting through to him. She was so sure he was on the straight-and-narrow. I started to feel a bit of sadness for her when she stopped and asked,

"Where did he get shot?" I said, "In the chest." She looked so surprised and asked as plain-as-day, "Wasn't he wearing his bulletproof vest?" I'll admit this threw me for a loop. How straight-and-narrow is the path you're on if you're known to commonly wear a bulletproof vest for protection at 16-years-old?

Have you ever found drug-filled balloons in someone before? If so, did they die from an overdose when one burst?

Sort of...they were drug-filled condoms. He did overdose, but none of the packs had burst. I think he was just using too much. Anyway, body-packing is never a good idea. Just, no. Don't do it.

How do you determine if a death was caused by accidental drug overdose or suicide?

Generally you can tell from the levels of drugs in their blood. An intentional overdose will have super high levels of one or two different drugs, where an accidental overdose generally has an elevated level of several drugs that are high (the levels won't be exorbitantly high, but at an increased, maintained level). Based on the levels, you can tell if a lifestyle sort of drug and the combination of medicine, or the long duration of use, caused the overdose. If we truly don't know whether it was a suicide or overdose, we would hold a coroner's inquest and a jury would decide. If they're unable to decide based on testimony and evidence given then it would be ruled "undetermined." (That ruling can be changed if new information is discovered a later date.) It's sort of like the cause of death comes directly from the body and the manner of death comes directly from the scene interpretation.

Are medical error deaths common?

I haven't encountered very many. There was a lady in a nursing home who was choking on her dinner. She had DNR (do not resuscitate) orders so the nurses and aides just put her to bed choking. They did put some oxygen on her though, so, that was helpful, I'm sure... Helpful in a taunting, "Hey, look at all this extra oxygen I bet you wish you could have!" sort of way. (Insert eye roll.) That was definitely medical error. That case was actually inquested and ruled accidental by the jury. The staff at the nursing home didn't have proper understanding of the DNR orders and what circumstances they covered. Additional training and clarification of DNR procedures were ordered and no charges were filed. I'm not sure if that family ever pursued filing civil charges against the nursing home, but I don't believe they did.

Choking is a very common concern for parents. Do you see many choking-related deaths?

Aside from the lady in the hospital, I've seen one child who was 5-years-old choke on a broken piece of latex balloon. Balloons are dangerous. Only go for Mylar if kids are actually going to play with them. This kid was 5! It happens!

My son didn't die, thank God, but at 8-months-old he choked on a push pin he'd found on the floor and eventually swallowed it. Here's the reason I'm not a first responder: I'm horrible in emergencies! After I found him choking I scooped him up, which caused him to swallow the pin, then ran out of the room screaming (both of us) and banged his head into the door frame, which led to more screaming...Yeah, I don't do well with emergencies. Much better being in the secondary level of response. With babies, it's very important to know the difference between choking and gagging when eating. Don't interfere with gagging. Let them work it out. It's safer.

Have you seen many other easily avoidable deaths?

Definitely with children; a couple were car seat-related and one was a drowning. An 18-month-old child was killed due to improper car seat use. She was in a car seat and the straps were too loose. When they crashed, she came out of the car seat and went through the open moon roof. She was hit by a car coming in the opposite direction. The other one happened when a baby was left to sleep in a car seat on a bed. At some point she kicked and tipped the car seat over and suffocated on the mattress.

I had a case where 9-month-old twins drowned in the bathtub because the dad ran downstairs to get something. It was especially tragic because normally the kids would've been at daycare, but this day, the dad took off work and stayed home with them. He was a mess. He punched holes in the walls, and at the hospital he tried to take the babies back and leave with them. It was so sad. Our gut reaction is to say, "Serves you right, you don't leave your kids in the tub unattended." But to see the parents so distraught, all you can do is offer sympathies. Accidents happen. As parents, we just need to be educated and extra vigilant in trying to avoid them.

Another tragic case that stands out in my mind is one involving a 4-year-old girl. I remember this particular case for many reasons: the fact it was a young child, the sad situation surrounding her death and knowing that she undoubtedly suffered. She was the daughter of low-income hard-working immigrants who literally worked around-the-clock to care for their family. Dad worked all day then came home to care for the kids while mom went to a part-time night job at a local industrial drycleaner. On this particular day, dad had come home sick, so mom, as she'd done sometimes in the past, brought the kids with her to work. They would just run around and play while mom worked. It wasn't uncommon for other employees to bring their children as well. On this particular evening, the children were playing "ride on the conveyor belt" which seemed to be a delightfully popular game. It was normal. It was fun. The little girl was standing at the end of the machine and the conveyor belt caught the sleeves of her shirt. Her arms were twisted and pulled into it, causing her to become stuck with her head pushed back and her neck against the machine. The force of the machine crushed her windpipe. She couldn't even scream. It all happened in a matter of seconds but some time had passed before the adults were able to successfully free her from the machine. Valiant efforts were made to save that sweet girl's life, but, alas, were futile. I can picture her right now, laying on the hospital gurney, her little arms all twisted, but just as angelic and peaceful-looking as ever. This poor child was so young and innocent. She was just playing. Accidental deaths like that seem extraordinarily tragic. I think it's because there seems to be no rhyme or reason to them happening.

MOTOR VEHICLE DEATHS

The Insurance Institute for Highway Safety and reports, "There were 30,057 fatal motor vehicle crashes in the United States in 2013 in which 32,719 deaths occurred."[i] The real question is: what is causing these crashes? There are obviously a variety of reasons accidents happen. Road conditions, vehicle malfunctions, and driver errors were studied by the National Highway Traffic Safety Administration. The report titled, "National Motor Vehicle Crash Causation Survey" outlines and analyzes the variables involved in motor vehicle crashes. It's important to determine the primary, or critical, reason behind a crash:

"In cases where the researchers attributed the critical reason to the driver, about 41 percent of the critical reasons were recognition errors (inattention, internal and external distractions, inadequate surveillance, etc.). In addition, about 34 percent of the critical reasons attributed to the driver were decision errors (driving aggressively, driving too fast, etc.) and 10 percent were performance errors (overcompensation, improper directional control, etc.). The researchers also made an assessment of other factors associated with the crash, such as interior non-

SPOILER ALERT: YOU'RE GONNA DIE

45

driving activities. In fact, about 18 percent of the drivers were engaged in at least one interior non-driving activity. The most frequent interior non-driving activity was conversation, either with other passengers in the vehicle or on a cell phone, especially among young (age 16 to 25) drivers. Among other associated factors, fatigued drivers were twice as likely to make performance errors as compared to drivers who were not fatigued."[ii]

It's clear that driver error plays a major role in causing car accidents and costing lives. Things like driving under the influence of drugs and alcohol, using handheld devices while driving and improper use of car safety equipment are a few major causes of the fatal accidents Jacquie encounters.

Do you get called to a lot of car accident deaths?

Yes, I've been to numerous car accidents in my career. I want to talk very personally about car accidents for a moment because I feel like this type of death rules my life. Obviously, no one plans on getting in a car accident. That's why it is, in fact, a car accident. But unlike most deaths, I feel that dying in a car crash is a genuine possibility for me and is one cause of death that is out of my control. I don't use illicit drugs, I rarely drink but a fruity cocktail every now and again, I don't abuse prescription medications, I stay active, etc. Those are decisions in my control that help me avoid the possibility of related deaths. The one thing I have very little control over is what other people do, and my biggest risk, every day, is driving in my car. This job has made me acutely aware that every single morning, when I drop my kids off at school, I may not make it back to pick them up. I feel like I give a little bit of my heart to each family member I encounter as I tell them that their loved one was killed in an accident. I'm aware that it just as easily could've been me, and that I'm alive only by the Grace of God.

It's a cruel, cruel reality that children aren't immune from tragic death. The best you can hope for is prevention. This is why seatbelts, car seats and booster seats matter and why people are so adamant about using them properly. This is why work trucks and vans often have a cage-type divider between the back and the driving compartment, because no one wants a hammer coming at them at 55 miles per hour. This is why proper tires, brakes, and regular car maintenance matters, because you don't need mechanical defects or problems while you're traveling down the highway. Awareness of your surroundings is key. Every state distributes a book with the annual numbers of vehicle-related fatalities broken down by gender, age, driver, passenger, motorcycle, pedestrian, etc. These accidents happen every single day and most people are blissfully unaware, while others unfortunately, don't get that same luxury. These people are forced to deal with the fact that a completely random, most likely completely avoidable accident has cost a loved one their life. There's just no coming back from that reality. And this is why it's so important that we all do our best to avoid making decisions that have the potential to cost lives.

Do seatbelts actually make a significant difference in a car accident?

I absolutely believe seatbelts make a difference in car crashes. And improper safety belt use is just as bad as not using one at all. I've seen a child transected at the waist due to improper safety belt use. She was in the back seat, with her seat belt on. The belt didn't fit well so she had the shoulder strap tucked behind her and she was only secured by the lap belt. Although she was above the minimum booster seat requirements, it was clear a regular seatbelt didn't fit properly, so she could've remained in a booster or used an adapter to help the belt fit properly. I think about this family, and the possibly avoidable outcome, all the time. Both this girl and her grandmother died in the crash. Her sister, who was sitting next to her, miraculously survived but needed many facial reconstructive surgeries. I called the dad this past October on the anniversary date of the accident to see how he was and let him know I still think of them.

The media emphasizes child car seat safety and standards. Do you think all of these rules and recommendations actually make a life vs. death difference?

My simple answer is yes; improper use of car seats really can make a critical difference. Going back to the 18-month-old child thrown out of the moon roof of the car during an accident, we can obviously never know what the outcome would've been had things been different, but the car seat straps being too loose certainly made it easier for her to be ejected from the vehicle. Had the straps been tightened to the proper recommendations, with only a finger-width of space between the shoulder and strap, she may have never come out of the car seat. That alone could have saved her life. There are rules and recommendations in place for a reason. I truly believe they can make all the difference.

There is a lot of talk and research about rear-facing vs. forward-facing car seats and the standards for appropriate age and weight a child should be for each position. I will say that I haven't encountered an accident in which the outcome would have been markedly different had a child been rear-facing vs. forward-facing. This doesn't mean that it doesn't happen or isn't important. The research has been done and I trust the conclusions. I'm just more familiar with deaths related to improper use and installation of car seats.

Do you encounter a lot of automobile airbag deaths?

Most accidents I see where someone has died and the airbag has been deployed are bad enough that the airbag wasn't to blame. I do know that airbag deaths do happen. I had an entire training on them, but I have yet to see one. The second generation airbags are so much better!

Do you come across a lot of intoxicated driving?

I've had numerous accidents where drugs or alcohol were involved in some capacity. Statistically, drunk driving is decreasing. There's been a lot of publicity and education about the ramifications of driving drunk and it's clear that the efforts are paying off. However, driving while under the influence of illegal and prescription drugs is increasing. I will say this: I can tell when I approach an accident (where drugs and/or alcohol are involved) whether the person at fault is drunk or high on marijuana simply based on the scene in front of me. Every. Single. Time. When alcohol is involved there seems to be an obvious loss of control that presents in some form at the scene. Whether the person at fault has crossed the center line, hit the gravel off the side of the road, overcorrected or missed a turn going at a high speed, I can see when the influence of alcohol had something to do with it.

Now, when marijuana is involved, I can just as easily see the evidence of it based on the scene in front of me. Usually the person at-fault has done something that is so ridiculously, obviously wrong. Time perception is heavily altered under the influence of marijuana and people seem to think they have way more time than actually necessary to do things. For example, I've seen cases where someone has come to a T-intersection, stopped, looked and then proceeded right in front of an oncoming semi-truck. They clearly thought they had enough time to pass in front of the semi. So, legalize marijuana, don't legalize it, I don't care. Just don't drive under the influence of drugs or alcohol. It's no good. Period.

SUNNY DAY SUICIDES:

We know the reasons people decide to take their own lives vary tremendously. One factor cannot be attributed as the sole cause of all suicides. However, there are theories that correlate increases in suicide to certain factors. A study was published in *JAMA Psychiatry* that compared 69,462 suicides that occurred in Austria between 1970 and 2010 to hours of sunshine during that day. The authors of the study concluded that:

"Duration of daily sunshine was significantly correlated with suicide frequency independent of season, but effect sizes were low. Our data support the hypothesis that sunshine on the day of suicide and up to 10 days prior to suicide may facilitate suicide. More daily sunshine 14 to 60 days previously is associated with low rates of suicide. Our study also suggests that sunshine during this period may protect against suicide." [iii]

How does this correlation to the date translate to the cause of suicides?

"It has been proposed that the effects of sunshine on mood and motivation in depressed patients are similar to those of antidepressants, by improving motivation and, only later, mood. Susceptible persons may become agitated and impulsive while still having depressed mood, which could lead to an increased suicide risk. Suicide attempts, although relatively rare, have also been described in patients with seasonal depression during the early stage of bright light therapy. In the long term, however, sunshine, similar to antidepressants, improves mood and thereby may contribute to decreased suicide. In sum, data indicate that due to interaction with the serotonergic system, sunshine influences mood, impulsiveness, and aggression, which are known to play a key role in suicidal behavior." [iv]

The "why" behind suicide will always be a big question, especially for those who have suffered a loss of someone this way. Unfortunately Jacquie has a lot of experience with this manner of death and was able to provide us with a little bit of insight her experiences have given her.

Does the theory of Sunny Day Suicides ring true for you?

The theory that sunshine, or lack thereof, plays a role in suicide is agreeable to me. I've seen the correlation in cases I've been involved with. I have a bit of a different theory, that sort of fits in with the "sunny day" studies. In my mind, having days of bad weather (lack of sunshine) makes everyone feel a little down or blue. It seems that a person suffering from depression sort of "fits in" and feels more normal during those because everyone around them is feeling down, too. Then, when the weather turns and the sunshine hits, most people's moods improve. My thought is that depressed person feels out of place and not quite "right" again because their mood didn't bounce back with the weather change like everyone else's. Those feelings are often extremely irrational and hard to understand, but suicide appears to be a very irrational decision.

Do most people leave suicide notes?

A common misconception is that people leave suicide notes. The reality is that most people do NOT leave a note. In these cases, the family is left completely crippled with the "why." "Why did they do it? Why didn't they talk to me? Why didn't they say anything? Why did they make plans for the weekend? Why did they schedule x, y or z if they were just planning on this? Why? Why? Why?" Depending on the circumstances, I attempt to offer answers. For instance, I might explain to a family member who is struggling, that suicide is often a very impulsive decision and that if the person had waited another 10 minutes they may not have actually gone through with it. I also explain that suicide can be very irrational and that they'll never be able to understand it. You can't rationalize something completely irrational. You will never have your answer. The peace to be had in these types of situations is to come to terms with the fact that you'll never know why. For whatever reason, in that second, that's the choice the person made and no amount of begging, no amount of money, no amount of good deeds, no amount of anything can change it or answer those questions. It's a terrible place to be and I feel so much sorrow for the family members who find themselves in that situation.

What are the "common" reasons for suicide that you've encountered?

I've seen many suicides in young teens who simply don't have the emotional maturity to understand that things will get better in their lives. I touched on this before, but teens are large children, not small adults. I really think if people could grasp that concept, we would be able to manage our teens a little better. They need rules and consistency and love and nurturing. Not freedom to make all of their own choices. They still need and seek guidance.

I've seen suicides of the elderly who have terminal illnesses that they would rather not suffer through or don't want their family to have to handle. I believe these individuals simply have misguided judgments with good intentions. I cannot recall a single family member who was glad that their mom or dad took their own life as opposed to trying to fight through their illness.

A common denominator in many suicides seems to be relationship issues. So, let's say a husband and wife are going through a bitter divorce (or any breakup, really) and one person commits suicide. The person who remains is often blamed, judged, shamed and cut off from the family. It's incredibly sad because the person left behind usually harbors a ton of guilt associated with the suicide and shouldn't be blamed for the actions of the person who committed the act. It's almost as if the person who commits suicide is given a dose of compassion and understanding for the decision they made. Yet the other victims, those left behind, aren't extended that same understanding. I see a lot of misplaced anger. I've counseled families that have started down that "blame path." I tell them they need to consider whether or not they want future relationships with their family, because suicide will often tear a family apart. Especially when you start passing blame on those around you. That being said, I've been able to experience suicides bringing families closer together. Families that have been fraught with conflicts over various things often break apart and after they have something tragic like a suicide amongst them, it sends everyone a wakeup call. They realize there are more important things in life than whatever pulled them apart in the first place.

Have you ever dealt with a murder-suicide situation?

I had one case that we ruled a murder-suicide. This was involving an elderly couple who were in advanced stages of failing health. They had no children, no siblings, or anyone nearby. Only each other. Due to their health issues, they were knocking on the nursing home door, a place neither of them wanted to be.

So, on this particular morning, the husband and wife got up out of bed and went into the garage where there were two kitchen chairs. They sat in the chairs and perhaps reminisced about their lives and exchanged their feelings of love for one another. Then, the husband got up, walked around behind the wife and pointblank shot her in the back of the head. This caused her to slump or fall off the chair. He gently laid her on the floor and covered her with a blanket. He then went back inside the home, retrieved some documents from the file where they were kept and placed them on the table. (We know he did this afterwards because the paperwork had the wife's blood on it.) He then pressed and activated the life-alert button on the necklace he wore. He removed the necklace, placed it on the table and went back into the garage. After lying down on the floor next to his wife's body, he placed the same gun in his mouth, pulled the trigger and shot himself. Meanwhile, the life alert was notifying the company, which made several attempts to contact the home without success. The life alert company proceeded to call 9-1-1 which then dispatched paramedics, the fire department, and police to the home. There, they made the grim discovery of the two bodies on the floor of the garage.

I like to think of this case as a sad love story of two people who couldn't stand the thought of losing each other. They needed to die together. But, of course, I'll never know if that was the true scenario that morning. The reality is, the wife could've had no clue of her husband's plan and may not have been a willing participant at all. It's much easier for me to believe the first scenario though, and I do believe they're together somewhere.

SIDS

The CDC reports:

"About 3,500 U.S. infants die suddenly and unexpectedly each year. We often refer to these deaths as sudden unexpected infant death (SUID). Although the causes of death in many of these children can't be explained, most occur while the infant is sleeping in an unsafe sleeping environment.

Researchers can't be sure how often these deaths happen because of accidental suffocation from soft bedding or overlay (another person rolling on top of or against the infant while sleeping). Often, no one sees these deaths, and there are no tests to tell sudden infant death syndrome (SIDS) apart from suffocation. To complicate matters, people who investigate SUIDs may report cause of death in different ways and may not include enough information about the circumstances of the event from the death scene.

Law enforcement, first responders, death scene investigators, medical examiners, coroners, and forensic pathologists all play a role in carrying out the case investigation.

A thorough case investigation includes:

• An examination of the death scene.

- An autopsy (medical examination of the body after death).

- A review of the infant's medical history.

Most SUIDs are reported as one of three types of infant deaths:

Sudden Infant Death Syndrome (SIDS)

SIDS is defined as the sudden death of an infant less than 1 year of age that cannot be explained after a thorough investigation is conducted, including a complete autopsy, examination of the death scene, and a review of the clinical history. SIDS is the third leading cause of infant deaths in the United States and the leading cause of death in infants 1 to 12 months old.

Unknown Cause

The sudden death of an infant less than 1 year of age that cannot be explained because a thorough investigation was not conducted and cause of death could not be determined.

Accidental Suffocation and Strangulation in Bed

Mechanisms that lead to accidental suffocation include:

- Suffocation by soft bedding, such as a pillow or waterbed mattress.

- Overlay—when another person rolls on top of or against the infant while sleeping.

- Wedging or entrapment—when an infant is wedged between two objects such as a mattress and wall, bed frame or other furniture.

- Strangulation, such as when an infant's head and neck become caught between crib railings.

Even after a thorough investigation, it is hard to tell SIDS apart from other sleep-related infant deaths such as overlay or suffocation in soft bedding. While an observed overlay may be considered an explained infant death, no autopsy tests can tell for certain that suffocation is the cause of death."ᵛ

As parents, the fear of a SIDS-related death weighs heavily. We're inundated with stories and conflicting information regarding infant deaths and safe versus unsafe sleep practices. Many of us had questions regarding SIDS deaths and Jacquie's experience with infant losses.

What are your thoughts on SIDS? I've heard that some medical examiners refuse to list it as a cause of death, which changes the statistics.

I would say SIDS is the least commonly used cause of death that I've seen used for infants. SIDS is a diagnosis of exclusion. So, when every other cause of death has been eliminated it is the "go to" diagnosis. It's a hard one for several reasons. It doesn't really provide any real explanations, and that's so hard on families. A SIDS diagnosis is sometimes given when something else is truly the cause of death but an official doesn't want to make someone feel bad. (Asphyxiation due to layover from unsafe bed-sharing, for example). There are some medical examiners who won't ever use SIDS as a diagnosis and simply put "undetermined" instead. Technically, it's the same cause of death as SIDS, but using the unclassified label leaves the option to change it later if new information is brought to light. As you can see, there's no national standard for this diagnosis, which makes it tricky to really evaluate.

If we suspect a SIDS diagnosis, there is a large amount of information we must collect and submit to the Illinois Department of Public Health. This information is used for research, statistics, etc. Our knowledge and understanding of SIDS is improving but the system isn't perfect. I know medical examiners don't get much say in the parenting world, but, for what it's worth, they would advise the following: Put babies on their backs and in their own space. I've heard that many, many times.

Have you had many SIDS cases? Do you see any similar characteristics in the infants who die from it?

Yes, unfortunately, I've had to investigate deaths where the cause was initially listed as SIDS. However, we don't officially use that label very often. If we have a baby die while bed-sharing, bed-sharing will almost certainly be listed as part of the cause. SIDS won't be listed. Please realize the SIDS deaths are particularly difficult for me to answer questions about because there is no standard for when to use it as a diagnosis. Where I'm located it is never, or rarely, used. If there truly is nothing that can be found, we would use sudden unexplained death of a child (SUDC) as the official cause of death.

I think the reports of the SIDS rates declining are a bit misleading in the fact that we just don't use SIDS as a cause of death very often anymore. That and the fact that many SIDS deaths from the past wouldn't actually be considered SIDS deaths nowadays. For example, if a baby were to die while bed-sharing, and everything else was ruled out, we would most likely put something like: asphyxia while bed-sharing; asphyxiation due to layover while bed-sharing; positional asphyxia due to wedging in bed space, etc., whereas years ago it would've simply been listed as SIDS. Another factor to consider is that every doctor uses SIDS diagnoses differently. A lot has to do with the training, experience, and knowledge of the doctor. That knowledge, combined with a complete and thorough investigation by us as death investigators, and the police and their investigations, are compiled for any death and especially a death of a baby. Again, the safest sleep for babies (according to the medical examiners) is on their backs and in their own space. Period. As for the second part of your question: no. We don't see any similar characteristics in these deaths. There are no correlating defects in the heart, brain or lungs or anything else. If we did, we would be all over that!

Even with all the information and recommendations, do you personally bed-share?

With my husband! I don't bed share with my kids (as infants). Each family has to evaluate that risk for themselves. But, I will say this: In all the infant deaths I have had to investigate, I have never (NEVER) had a case involving a baby dying in their crib. I know it happens, but, I've never seen it. That means a lot to me.

Bed-sharing advocates often say when done correctly--firm mattress, no pillows or blankets near baby, no drugs or alcohol, no bed-sharing when overtired, no gaps between mattresses and headboard or wall, and keeping baby with mom only (no siblings in bed)--that bed-sharing is safe. Have you personally seen one or more of these "no-no's" in bed-sharing deaths?

Yes! There's always been an element of unsafe sleep practices in the infant deaths I've encountered. I've seen intoxicated (in one form or another) parents in bed with babies; siblings in bed with babies, babies wedged between the wall and the bed, babies wedged between the mattress and headboard area, and a few others. Every parent has to decide what risks they're willing to take and what they're comfortable with. I would never make a blanket statement like, "don't bed-share," because millions of families do it without issue. Regardless of your decisions, parenthood is simply a matter of staying consistent and vigilant, because letting your guard down, even once, could be deadly.

A NOTE FROM JACQUIE

I know this section was packed with a lot of information. If I could just address other professionals in the death industry for a moment: I realize that some of my answers may not be exactly spot-on. So many things vary by regions, standard practices, etc. I imagine other people in this industry reading through this and having the same reaction I do to watching an episode of *CSI*, which is essentially foaming-at-the-mouth, seizure-type screaming. Please know that I'm not oblivious to this fact. I bet someone has been reading up until this point screaming, "That's not what we do!" And I get it. But, please know that I'm responding based on my personal experiences and education. I've pared my answers down in the simplest way possible to provide a general understanding. If you want to discuss specifics, write your own book! (Or call me!)

THE BODY

WE KNOW OUR own bodies and their specific functions pretty well. However, the changes that occur starting at the moment of death all the way through to the decomposition process are something most of us won't ever see for ourselves. I'm not going to pretend I haven't ever wondered a weird thing or two about corpses. Come on, you know you have, too! To my relief, others had the same, if not even odder, questions that I did. (For the record, it's been established that dead guys don't get boners. This question was asked so many times I figured I'd put it here, in the beginning, so you no longer have to live your life without knowing that critical piece of information. You're welcome.) If you're feeling down because you've never had the whole "been-in-a-room-with-a-corpse" experience, don't worry. Jacquie has seen, smelled, and even once tasted enough for all of us. She has graciously spared us from living our woefully ignorant lives by answering pretty much every question thrown at her.

* * *

Can you describe what a decomposing body smells like?

Go to the store, buy a beef roast, and put it outside (protected from animals) in the heat. After a few days, go back and smell it. It's pretty much like that. Now, go buy a fresh beef roast, open the package and take a big whiff of the beef. That's about what it smells like during an autopsy.

Do you ever have to take a shower at work or change your clothes so that when you get home you don't reek of decomposition smell?

Though it doesn't happen very often, I've definitely had instances where I called home and had whoever was there meet me at the back door with my robe because my clothes were not coming in the house. If I've come in contact with roaches or other insects that can be spread, or if I've been at a particularly bad scene with a severely decomposed body, there is no way those clothes are coming in. There are many pieces of my job that I bring home with me. Insects and human flesh are not some of them.

I've heard Vicks® VapoRub™ in a face mask works to cover the smell of rotting bodies. Do you use that technique?

I rarely wear a face mask; in fact, I never wear one just to cover up the smell. Other people who can't stand the smell do use the Vicks and they say it works. I guess I'm just used to the smell or something because it doesn't bother me one bit.

True story: When I was in college, doing my practicals, I was sewing up this guy after I finished working on him. Well, the ligature I was using pulled through his skin so I had to start over and rethread my needle. I put the end of the ligature IN MY MOUTH to rethread it! You know, like I was about to sew a patch on a pair of pants or something, but instead it was human flesh. Ugh. It makes me want to vomit just thinking about it.

Can corpses really spontaneously sit up?

The simple answer is no. However, I can explain where this originated. When you embalm a person, the fluid you inject is very liquid. After a few hours the fluid will diffuse into the surrounding tissues and begin to harden. Similar to Jell-O gelatin, which begins as liquid and starts to harden, or "set up" after several hours. After a few hours in the fridge, you may say, "I made Jell-O and it set up very nicely." It isn't uncommon to hear an embalmer say to another, "I had a body set up nicely this morning." Thus, the misunderstanding of bodies "setting up" at funeral homes after they've died. If a funeral director and/or coroner had a body legitimately SIT UP, they would call for an ambulance, because that's not dead.

Why can't hospitals remove medical equipment/devices from corpses?

No devices can be removed from the body because we have to make sure every procedure was done correctly, and be able to evaluate any areas that could look like trauma from medical intervention. However, we've always been allowed by our medical examiners to take measures to hide any equipment as best as possible. We use little tricks like cutting off the end of the endotracheal tube and sticking it down inside the mouth a little, tying off any I.V.s and any other tubing and tucking them in as best as possible, so the family can see their loved one without all that stuff in the way. If you work in healthcare (ER, hospital, etc.) ask your coroners if they would be willing to do things like this. They should be able to leave everything in place but strategically tuck it out of sight.

How is time of death determined?

The official time of death is my on-scene time plus 1 minute. That's the time they're pronounced. I can roughly figure out how long someone's been dead based on a few things: rigor mortis, livor mortis, and algor mortis.

Rigor comes on in about 4-6 hours, peaks around 14-16 hours and is usually gone by about 24 hours. **Livor** is the blood pooling because it's no longer being pumped through the body. (It makes the purplish discolorations and varies based on different things.) **Algor** is the cooling of the body. Generally 4 degrees Fahrenheit the first hour and about 1.5 degrees for every hour after that until you reach room temperature. (This isn't very scientific and never officially used.)

I've heard your eyes kind of deflate when you die, since they're made mostly of water, and that they're sewn or superglued shut. Is this true?

The eyes do change after death. We've always used plastic eye caps. Also, we have something called "tissue builder" which can be injected under the skin in various little sneaky places. This gives the person a healthier look so they don't appear as sunken or emaciated. The eyelids are glued shut, yes, usually with a glue called Aron Alpha® Industrial Krazy Glue™. The mouth is generally closed with wire tacks and the lips are then glued with the Aron Alpha as well. There's a lot of work that goes into preparing someone for a funeral. We don't do any of this prep work at the morgue, though. The funeral home handles most of those details if the body is being viewed.

When someone's body is extremely damaged, and it's obvious the body can't be viewed, do they try to piece it together for viewing? What happens if it can't be made viewable?

Most often, when a person dies after suffering trauma extreme enough to render the body unviewable, the body is kept in a body bag. The funeral home will rarely try to "put it together." If the family sends clothes they're normally draped nicely on top of the body bag. That's sad, I know. But I do want to say that this is by no means the norm. I'm referring to the extreme cases of severe trauma. Most people can be at least partially prepared and dressed.

What do the lungs of a smoker look like?

They look pink with lots of black splotches on them.

What happens with the bodies of very premature infants that are born at home?

There are no specific laws governing a fetus born prior to 20 weeks (in Illinois, anyway). It's usually up to the people involved as to what happens to a fetus that small. I had a case once involving a woman who had a miscarriage at 16 weeks. She delivered the fetus, put it in a box and buried it in her backyard. Years later she confided in a neighbor about it during a heart-to-heart-type conversation. Well, this neighbor decided to call the cops upon hearing her story. The police came, dug up the entire backyard, found the box, and then called me. I got on the phone with the officer in charge, asked a few questions, verified she was 16 weeks gestation, etc. I told him to very nicely fill the hole back in, make sure it looks nice, pay your respects and leave that woman and her baby alone. In another case a man called me and said that he and his wife had lost their unborn baby's heartbeat at the hospital. They decided to come home and let it pass naturally. She was delivering the baby and wanted to know what to do with it. I verified she was 18 weeks along and told them I would help anyway they wanted. I offered to come and get the baby, to have the baby cremated, that they could pretty much do whatever you would do with any other death. They ultimately went with cremation.

A NOTE FROM JACQUIE

I realize that what seems normal to me can actually be quite disturbing to people. I can recall the moment this realization truly hit me. I got to play the role of coroner in the movie *Eagle Eye*. I was tasked with fingerprinting, utilizing a handheld scanner, the finger of a charred body that was burned by falling electrical wires. (There was so much inaccuracy with everything, but hey, it's the movies.) Billy Bob Thornton and Ethan Embry were the FBI agents in the scene with me and many others (shout out to Kendall County Sheriff's Office and the Newark Fire Department!). Billy Bob Thornton asked me several questions about the body, and I answered him with the same direct, straight-forward and honest answers I gave for this book. His response involved a choice curse word and genuine disgust. I figure if I can gross out a man who's been known to wear a vial of blood around his neck (on purpose!), then I must have true macabre immunity.

THE AUTOPSY

NOT EVERYONE makes it to the morgue, and even fewer have an autopsy completed. Without cause, a body is quickly released to the funeral home for the next step of the process. After learning the ins and outs of an autopsy, I couldn't really decide if I would want one done or not, and I'm relieved I don't get to cast a real vote on the decision when the time comes. On one hand, the thought of someone sawing through my bones makes me a little queasy. Then there's also the whole lying naked on a table thing. I mean, I know I'll be dead and all, but I'm pretty convinced that when I die I'll be totally commando, with burly unshaven lumberjack legs, accompanied by extremely unkempt nails and crusted chocolate residue plastered all over my face. (Not a day goes by that I don't savagely devour *something* chocolate. At least they'll know I died happy.) I'd really prefer as few people as possible to witness that horror show. On the other hand, autopsies are pretty friggin' amazing. Someone is literally investigating the inside of you, communicating with your body and helping piece together the last story it will ever tell. If I do end up requiring an autopsy, I hope I'm at least half as interesting as the autopsies Jacquie told us about.

* * *

Who decides when an autopsy should be performed?

Autopsies are done at the discretion of the coroner or deputy coroner. If there is sufficient information (either at the scene or via medical history) to establish a cause of death, and no evidence needs to be documented from the body, there probably won't be an autopsy. We have complete jurisdiction over a dead body. So, if the family doesn't want an autopsy, that's just too bad if we think it's necessary. Of course we explain that very nicely to them. (I mean, if I had just killed my husband and was given a say in the matter, I surely wouldn't be authorizing an autopsy. So, for obvious reasons, we retain that jurisdiction over the body.) Mostly though, I don't come across people refusing an autopsy, I get people who desperately want me to request an autopsy. I sometimes have to tell them no. I try to explain why an autopsy isn't necessary. If they really want one I will set it up and they can pay for it personally, but not at the taxpayers' expense.

Are there state requirements that dictate who gets autopsied? For instance, I was told in my state, if you die at home or pass within 24 hours after being released from the hospital, autopsies are automatically done.

Each state has its own requirements. You can look up your state statutes that govern coroners; it will be listed there. Where I'm located, the only required autopsies are: any death where there are questionable or suspicious circumstances, deaths in police custody (or deaths during police chase/pursuit), and a cause of death that cannot be reasonably determined except by autopsy.

How much does an autopsy cost?

The cost of an autopsy varies, but for us it's about $1,200 and is paid by the county funds. For a family paying directly for a private autopsy, it would probably be about $2,500. I've seen cheaper and more expensive, depending on the circumstances. These are numbers that reflect what I see in our area; the numbers fluctuate substantially by geographical area.

Can you explain how an autopsy is performed?

The body is completely prepped or cleaned with soap and water. An incision is made from the corner of the shoulders to the middle of the breastbone, sort of like a V-shape. Then, from the bottom of the V, a straight incision is made from the breastbone to the pubic bone, creating a Y-shaped incision. Then those flaps of skin are pulled back. The intestines are removed and put into the viscera bag.[4] The chest plate (breastbone and front part of ribs) is removed and placed aside. The heart, lungs, spleen, kidneys, liver, pancreas are removed, (the uterus is removed on a female and the prostate is checked from the inside on a man), then the stomach is removed and emptied. Each organ is weighed, dissected, photographed if needed, documented and then placed into the viscera bag. The tongue, larynx, pharynx, esophagus, trachea, and aorta are removed, kind of all together as one large unit, then dissected, photographed, and placed into the viscera bag.

An incision is made in the scalp from ear-to-ear over the top of the head. The scalp is peeled forward and downward. The calvarium (top of the skull consisting of parts of the frontal, parietal, and occipital bones) is removed. The brain is removed, weighed, dissected, photographed, and placed in the viscera bag. The empty cavities of the body (chest, abdomen, and head) are examined for any injury. The viscera bag is sealed and placed back inside the abdomen. The chest plate is replaced on top of that. The three flaps of skin are brought back together and sutured closed. The calvarium is placed back on top of the head; the scalp is

---

[4] *A viscera bag is approximately the size of a 13-gallon garbage bag (more square though) and made of a thick plastic material. It lines a 5-gallon bucket during the autopsy when it's filled with the organs being removed. The entire bag and its contents are sealed and returned to the body after the autopsy is complete.*

folded back to its original shape and sutured. The body is placed into a body bag and is then released to the funeral home.

Depending on the doctor and/or technician doing the eviscerating of the organs, the order in which the organs are removed will vary. Sometimes, the death circumstances will dictate the order that the organs are examined. For instance, I used to work with a pathologist who always examined the offending or suspected organ last. So, if the doctor, based on the information available, believed the cause of death would be cardiac-related, he always examined the heart last. This ensured he wouldn't miss anything important while going through the motions of completing the autopsy.

So, essentially, the body is opened, the organs are individually removed, examined, photographed, and then returned to the body in a viscera bag. That's the nuts and bolts of it anyway. Oh, and the final closure (usually done at the funeral home) is called a baseball stitch because the body is closed using the same stitching that you see on a baseball.

What do you do with the bodily fluids?

They are flushed or rinsed down the drain just like all your other bodily fluids.

I'm curious about breast implants...Are they usually removed?

We try very hard to avoid them if we can during an autopsy. Even to the point we do a U-incision versus the traditional Y-incision to prevent slicing them. They just leak everywhere and some of the older ones are very, very sticky.

Have you ever had a body explode on you? (Like, it's super swollen and you cut into it and it erupts all over?)

Yes, I've had a body (or two, or three, or four) "explode" (your word, not mine!) on me from being decomposed. It's nasty. And, as a bonus, their skin sticks to you. It's really tough to get it off.

Do you judge hairy people? Like a woman with unshaved legs?

Yes.

Great. Now when I start shaving everyday my husband is going to think it's because I want sex. Do you think I'll get away with telling him I'm only shaving in case I die?

You can tell him... But it won't matter. He'll still want to have sex with you. I'm sorry.

What do you do when you get a body of a pregnant woman? Do you leave the baby in the mother? Or do you have to do a separate autopsy on the baby? Is the baby removed for its own cremation, burial etc.?

Ugh....if we're working with a mother who has died while pregnant we'll remove the baby as part of the autopsy. It's very sad. Whether or not we autopsy the baby depends on the mother's cause of death. If mom died of natural disease we won't (usually) autopsy the baby. If mom died of a gunshot wound or something, then we will, because they often can prosecute for the death of the baby as well and that evidence will need to be gathered for the case.

I can remember arguing, for lack of a better word, about this with the doctor performing the autopsy. (I won.) This poor woman died at 38 weeks pregnant from a dissecting aorta of pregnancy. It was so sad. Anyway, I remember taking this sweet baby (a girl) from the mother. The doctor I was working with suggested we autopsy the baby as well, but I told him no. We knew why the baby died and there was no reason whatsoever to do an autopsy on her. I called the dad and asked if he wanted to see her. I wrapped her in a blanket and the dad came up and held her. It was so sweet and so heartbreaking. She was buried in the casket with her mother.

How closely do you inspect a body? Will any marks (like needle marks, bruising, or anything) become more apparent to the naked eye after death?

It really depends. Each body we're called in for is examined at the scene. The presenting scene will dictate how much examination we do. For instance, a car accident victim will get a much more thoroughly documented body exam than a person with a long history of cancer who died in bed. After that examination we determine if an autopsy is needed. If we do an autopsy, then each body, regardless of the cause of death, is thoroughly examined. Every tattoo, scar, obvious birthmarks, and so forth, is documented. If there are a lot of external injuries such as bruises, abrasions, lacerations, etc., those will be documented as well. The body is usually photographed as a whole, then in thirds and finally each specific mark, injury, tattoo, etc. Everything, right down to whether or not the toenails are clean or dirty, is noticed and documented. To answer the second part, yes, sometimes some bruising and marks become much more apparent after death.

Are you more careful with a body that will be buried knowing it's likely they'll be viewed versus a body you know will be cremated?

We treat all bodies very carefully, as if they will be viewed. Sometimes families change their minds about cremation or want do a viewing before cremation. All bodies are treated as if they will have an open casket viewing.

Do you photograph all autopsies?

The autopsies are generally photographed by a police evidence technician (a real CSI!). However, if no police are present for the autopsy, then yes, we document the autopsy with photos.

How many hours does the average autopsy take?

The average autopsy, without having to gather evidence, takes about 45 minutes. With a lot of injury to document or evidence to gather, they can take up to 4 or 5 hours. We schedule about 2 hours for each autopsy, from start to cleaned morgue finish. I remember once we worked for nearly 2 hours trying to find a projectile that was lodged in a hip bone. We worked and worked. Went back to the x-rays, went back to the body, made more cuts in the hip bone, kept searching for this projectile. We could see it on the x-ray so we knew it was in there. After about 2 hours, we were looking at the x-ray yet again, scratching our heads (figuratively, not literally). Finally it dawned on us that the x-ray was backwards and we'd been looking in the wrong hip the entire time. We went to the other hip bone and found it in about 1 minute. Ha! Lesson learned.

Is it a different experience to work on an obese corpse as opposed to someone of average weight? If so, how does it affect the process?

Yes, in that it generally takes more than just one person to assist. Also, depending on the size of the person, we may have to change our procedures a bit. We've had a couple of bodies that were too big to fit in our cooler drawers so we had to transport them to another county with a walk-in cooler. The biggest difference, though, is just in moving the body.

Has a body ever "woke up" on you?

Yes... My husband! But in all seriousness, no, I've never had that experience (thank God!).

Are body bags disposable or do they get re-used?

I can't speak for other places, but, no, we do not reuse body bags. Ever. I'm sure a defense attorney would *love* to know if that was happening though...

What's the strangest item you've found in a body?

I found a remote control and a Snickers® bar, still in the wrapper, in the fat rolls of a really, really obese person. It was sort of uncomfortable having to give the remote back to the family. "Um... We found this..."

You gave the remote back, but what did you do with the Snickers bar?

I ate the Snickers bar.

THE OPTIONS

SO I'M PRETTY SURE we've made it clear (and if not, prepare yourself for some tough news) that you are guaranteed to die. And when that happens, aside from a rapture, your body will be left behind. It has to go somewhere, and now is a good time to start figuring out where you'd like that to be.

As it turns out, there are quite a few things you can do with a corpse. The options are practically limitless. For example, in addition to the choice of being buried traditionally, you can choose to be used as a cadaver in a classroom (yes, that's right, your dead body can lay naked, in a room full of college kids, ready to be used for some form of medical practice), your cremated remains can be pressed into a diamond, or you can be frozen until the end of time. And that's just the beginning. There really is something for everyone. We'll highlight all of the common options, as well as a few of the lesser-known choices. It's our hope that you use this information as a launching pad to help make some decisions and take action in the preparations for your death.

* * *

BURIAL

Burial after death is a very common ritual. Typically, a body is placed in a casket or coffin (usually with a burial vault or grave liner to prevent the grave from sinking) and buried in a cemetery. There are countless options as to where, what, and even who you are buried with. If you've made the decision to be buried, you'll want to find the place in which you would like to be buried, purchase a plot if necessary, find (and possibly purchase) a box or casket that suits you and decide if you would like to be buried with any personal items. Each cemetery has different guidelines, so you'll want to follow those once you choose a place. For those wondering, you generally cannot be buried on private property, but it is possible to establish family cemeteries in certain areas. Research the guidelines for your area. Headstones or grave markers are commonly used and can be purchased, and even placed, prior to your passing.

Natural, or green, burials are also available in certain areas. This is a process in which a body is buried directly into soil and will eventually decompose into the earth. Though not a very mainstream option, green burials are starting to increase in popularity. Just like traditional cemeteries, each company has their own set of guidelines and procedures. Be sure to familiarize yourself with these practices and submit requests ahead of time. For example, most people considering a green burial find joy in the fact that their body will decompose naturally and "give back" to nature. If an autopsy is completed when you die, the viscera bag with all your organs in it will be placed inside you as part of standard procedure at the morgue. If you are unhappy with the idea of the plastic bag decomposing in to the earth with you, you will need to make arrangements to have it removed prior to burial. A similar request should be discussed with, and arranged by, the company handling your green burial.

Do you really need to be buried in a casket or can they just throw your body in a hole?

If you're going to be buried in a cemetery, yes, you need a casket and burial vault for the casket to go into. Otherwise our cemeteries would be full of sunken graves. You can only be thrown into a hole if you are murdered...and even then it's only until you are found. There are green cemeteries where you can be wrapped in a shroud and placed in a hole; however, you may pay a significant premium for this because, believe it or not, the upkeep is much greater for this type of cemetery. More and more options for green burials are becoming available, and as with most things, there is a wide range of pricing. Some cost significantly less than others and each company will have their own method of completing the burial.

Has anyone been buried with their pet in the casket with them?

I know of one case where someone was buried with an actual animal. The animal died at the same time as its owner, at home, in a carbon monoxide accident. They were placed in the casket together. Other than that, I've seen people buried with the cremains of pets that have previously died.

Is it possible to be buried in your own family cemetery?

There is a way to do this if you can have someone file all the proper paperwork. Usually though, unless there's an existing family cemetery, no one does the work to create one. Look in to your state's requirements. If you would like to be buried on your own land, get the process started now.

When I die, am I allowed to be buried with my husband? Let's say he dies first, 5 years before me; could they dig him up and throw me in with him?

Probably. For the right amount of money you can pretty much do anything. I would imagine it to happen like this: Your husband dies and you purchase the largest casket you can buy for him to be buried in. Years later, you die. You're placed in a rented casket for your wake or funeral. Then the body of your husband is exhumed (which takes a separate order and authorization), your body is placed in with his, the casket is closed, resealed and put back into the vault. One stone could read both of your names. You wouldn't both fit nicely in there though, so you'll have to be okay with being jammed in there together. Personally, I couldn't imagine sharing a casket with my husband for eternity. I'd be all, "scoot over!"

If you really, truly want this to happen, make sure to make proper plans now. I'm sure it will be much harder for your family to carry out with you gone.

Now, if you aren't particular about physically being in the casket with your husband, you may have the option of being "double stacked." You would purchase a plot, and the first person to die would be buried around eight feet down, and the next person would be buried on top, about four feet down. Again, the options are almost endless, really. Do your research and find a company that will work with you to get exactly what you want.

It seems like people often complain about the cost of funerals, burials, and post-death costs in general. Is there a big markup? Is it as expensive as it seems?

There are definitely some shady funeral directors out there, as in most professions. However, I think the majority are pretty good about working within a family's means and finding what works for them. If you are looking for a really cheap casket, you won't see it on the showroom floor. You'll have to ask about a cloth-covered casket or a simple 18-gauge steel casket (most likely found in a catalog) and it will be much cheaper.

EMBALMING

Embalming is a method of preserving human remains by treating them with chemicals to delay decomposition. The intention is to keep them suitable for public display at a funeral, for religious reasons, or for medical and scientific purposes such as their use as anatomical specimens. The three goals of embalming are sanitization, presentation, and preservation (or restoration).[vi]

Can you explain the process of embalming?

A normal embalming goes like this: An incision is made right at the collarbone area on the right side of the body. The jugular vein and the carotid artery are found. A tube is put into the carotid artery and a small nick is made in the jugular vein. The tubing is connected to a pump that's filled with a water/formaldehyde solution. The pump is turned on and embalming fluid is pumped through the carotid artery, feeding through the rest of the body and as it pushes in the embalming fluid, the blood pours out of the nick in the jugular vein and drains on the table, which is slightly tilted downward. When the fluid has gone all the way through, the vessels are tied off, the incision is sutured up and that's pretty much it. There are some additional little things here and there, but that's the gist of it.

What do you do with the drained fluids?

Just like during an autopsy, they go down the drain.

Since embalming slows down the decomposition process, does the body look the same a long time after being buried? I've always been curious if their body looks the same when I visit loved ones' graves.

I don't know the exact number of years, and I'm sure there are varying factors, but, a normal well-embalmed body will remain pretty much the same for many, many, many (30+) years. There may be some slight decay or mold depending on the time and conditions, but overall the body should look like it did when it was buried. There was a case of a civil rights activist named Medgar Evers. He was murdered when his son was a very young boy. Before being buried he was embalmed. After 30 years or so they exhumed him and re-examined his body. He looked so amazing that they called his son and gave him the opportunity to come and see his remains.

Do embalmed bodies smell similar to un-embalmed bodies?

No. The un-embalmed body will start to have odor very shortly (hours to a day or two) after death. An embalmed body can be around for weeks without a major odor. It might not be as perfect as first day of embalming, but, it definitely won't smell the same as the un-embalmed body. Exhumed embalmed bodies smell a little more, depending on how long they have been buried, but not as badly as an un-embalmed body. In my opinion, anyway.

When someone dies with disfiguring wounds (gunshot to the head, traumatic car accident, and the like) how do you do the embalming? Wouldn't the fluid leak out?

We make things we call "packs" – essentially big wads of cotton soaked in embalming fluid – which we put in/on the wounds to dry them out. Then, we may do a 6-point injection (meaning we embalm the body through 6 points: each side of the neck, each arm and each leg separately). However, if someone has seriously disfiguring wounds to the point that they can't be viewed publicly, then the family often opts to not have embalming and the body is just placed in a sealed body bag and then inside the casket for burial.

I once viewed an embalmed corpse and noticed a plug in his belly through his shirt. It kind of looked like a pop-up turkey timer. What was the plug for?

It's from a step in the embalming process, usually the last step, and it's referred to as cavity work. There's an instrument called a trocar (kind of a long spear-like object that's hollow and connected to a tube with suction). We use this by inserting it in the stomach area and pushing it around to suction out any fluids left within the body (the cavities). After being used to suction, the same trocar is then attached to tubing and a bottle of cavity fluid (a higher concentrated embalming fluid) and the cavities are then embalmed using a gravity method. Then, after you remove the trocar, you put that plastic "plug" called a trocar button in its place.

Do you have to be embalmed?

No. You only have to be embalmed if you're going to have a public viewing, if your body will travel over state lines (unless it's within 24 hours of death) or if you die from bubonic plague, smallpox or cholera. The point is mainly to preserve the body for viewing and to ensure that there are no health hazards if the body is presented to the public. This is the law where I am. It differs from state-to-state. You'll also be required to be embalmed if your body is transported via common carrier (airplane, train, etc.)

I've heard that Jews don't embalm the dead. Do you often work with people's religious views?

Yes, that's true. We get the autopsy done within a few hours to respect the requirement of burial within 24 hours. For Jewish people, everything must stay with the body. Everything! I'm very respectful of people's religious beliefs when it comes to the bodies and do my best to make sure things are carried out according to their requests. I consider it part of my duties to make sure all this stuff happens properly!

CREMATION

"Contemporary cremation is a two-step taphonomic process that reduces a body to small bone fragments and ash. The remains are first cremated in a retort (crematorium oven) to reduce the body down to the inorganic fraction of bone. After the cremation cycle is completed, the cremated remains are removed from the retort and processed, or pulverized, in order to reduce the overall volume for either inurnment or scattering."[vii]

I've heard you don't "burn" when cremated because the flames never actually touch the body. Instead, the heat melts the flesh. Is this incorrect? Are the bodies actually burned?

Very high heat is used (I think around 1500°F). The flames do not touch the body. The body tissues and the bones do sort of incinerate, but you're left with larger pieces of large bones that have to be ground up afterwards. When it's all said and done, there's the ash, the remnants of incinerating (it's very much like dust), and the pieces of ground bone, which are all packaged up together.

Has anyone ever "woken up" while being cremated?

Well, we don't actually do the cremations here at the morgue so I can't say for sure. Our job is only to authorize cremations. In any case, no one should ever accidentally wake up just before cremation since they would've been thoroughly examined by us first. There's a pretty solid system of checks and balances to avoid mistakes of that nature.

Why are people cremated in boxes?

There are only a handful of crematories and they usually service several funeral homes and private cremation services. All of these different agencies will feed into one location for cremation and the crematory must maintain each individual and all of their specific belongings. The identifying information is on the box and the crematory can keep everyone straight without having bodies lying around. The bodies are also cremated with their clothing on and whatever else they may want with them (any of those items would be placed in the box).

A little off-topic, but this reminds me of the crematory in Georgia several years ago (2002) that let bodies pile up because their crematory was broken down. The families were receiving Quickrete (a concrete mix) and were told it was cremains[5]. Upon discovery, the only thing the crematory got in trouble for was fraudulent business practice or something like that because there were no laws governing the dead bodies. Thankfully, there are laws now.

Do you have to be cremated after an autopsy?

You do not have to be cremated after an autopsy. We take very special care to ensure the body is able to be open-casket viewed if the family wishes.

When someone is cremated are there rules for where they can be spread?

Technically, you aren't supposed to spread them anywhere. (But, hey, I won't look.) If someone wanted to be a jerk about it, they could push the issue and you could probably be fined or some other sort of legal action for spreading cremains. You're only supposed to bury them in cemeteries. A keen funeral director will simply ask you if you want the urn sealed or not. This is sort of code for "do you plan on spreading the ashes?" because if you do, you will not want the urn sealed.

What happens to things like rods, artificial hearts, and hip replacements when someone is cremated? Do they take them out even when they're so deep in the body? What if they didn't know the person had one?

I've only seen a couple of these circumstances. At the ones I've witnessed, the artificial piece is just added to the cremains. For example, after the body is removed from the retort where it was cremated, the metal pieces left behind are simply put in the cremation container and the cremains are added in around it. Certain devices, such as a

---

[5] *Cremains is a term widely used when referring to a persons cremated remains.*

pacemaker, have to be removed before cremation. It's actually part of the disclaimer that the family has to sign off. Without removal, these devices will explode during the cremation.

AFTER CREMATION

So, you're officially a jar of cremains. Now what? As it turns out, there are quite a few options in addition to the traditional urn-on-the-mantle setup. While there are literally hundreds of options, here are a few we found interesting:

- LifeGem is a company that turns the carbon in cremains or locks of hair into an authentic diamond. These diamonds can be made in various colors and can be used in all forms of jewelry just as a regular diamond would. The diamond can be made as little or big as you'd like. The smallest gem size starts at $2,490. [viii]

- A Bios Urn will turn you into a tree of your choice. This is currently an option for both people and pet cremains. "The seed germinates in the top capsule, separated from the ashes. Once the urn starts to biodegrade seed roots are already strong enough to contact the ashes. With biodegradation the entire set becomes part of the sub-soil." At $145 an urn this is a very cost-efficient and unique option. [ix]

- Eternal Reefs will use your ashes to preserve and protect the marine environment by casting your ashes into a cement structure and placing it in the bottom of the ocean. "An Eternal Reef combines a cremation urn, ash scattering, and burial at sea into one meaningful, permanent environmental tribute to life." The most basic Eternal Reef casting starts at $2,495.[x]

- Ever wanted to go to space? Celestis can send your cremains to space, as part of an actual space mission, starting at $1,295.[xi]

- Angels Flight will send you out with a bang. They load your cremains into fireworks and put on an entire display for your friends and family on their private yacht. Prices start at $4,250.[xii]

You really can do just about anything with cremains. If you know you would like to be cremated, take some time to think of how you'd like your cremains to be used!

ENTOMBMENT

You don't hear a lot about entombment these days. In fact, I never even knew it existed as an option until I saw it on the episode of *Keeping Up with the Kardashians* where Kris Jenner explored all of her burial options. (Obviously I was tuning in purely for educational purposes.) Mount Pleasant Group, a cemetery and funeral operation that provides above-ground options, explains the basics of entombment for us: "Entombment is the interment of human remains in a tomb or crypt, and today is most often referred to as above-ground burial. It involves placing a casket or cremation urn in a crypt or columbarium niche within a mausoleum. The crypt or niche is then sealed and a memorial is added."[xiii]

A mausoleum is a building used to house the remains of multiple people. Within the mausoleum are crypts. A casket is placed and sealed within the crypt. You can purchase a double crypt that will accommodate two caskets. A columbarium is a series of compartments or niches that house multiple levels of cremains. The niches are designed to hold urns full of cremains. A single, double, and family niche may be purchased and will be housed within the columbarium.

DONATION

Body donation is a unique way to have your body put to use after death. This option does require a bit of research and planning prior to death, so if you're considering it, start researching and make arrangements today. There are a few directions you can go with donation. First, there's organ, eye, and tissue donation. This decision allows your organs to be used for the benefit of another person, but allows your body to still be available for the other options (burial, cremation, etc.). It's important to register to be a donor online (www.organdonor.gov) or at the DMV when you renew your driver's license so that proper measures can be taken when the time comes.

A full-body donation sends your body to a medical or research facility of your choosing. Once deceased, you can be sent to a certain medical facility to be used in researching a particular disease or ailment. Your body can be sent to a facility where it will become a cadaver to educate students and allow for practice in their field, prior to working on live subjects. Doctors, nurses, dentist, physical therapists and others in the medical field use cadavers in the classroom. It's probably just my morbid curiosity, but this last option makes me want to visit and watch those cadavers being used! Kind of.

The University of Tennessee's Forensic Anthropology center accepts body donations and uses them to study various means of body decomposition. For those who want to just be thrown in a hole to rot, this one's for you! This place – widely known as a "Body Farm" – was the first of its kind to stage bodies in various environments, conditions, etc., and then study the decomposition and other variables. (I found the Body Farm so interesting that I dedicated a chapter to it. I have to give you some sort of incentive to stick with this book!) And yes, you can visit. However, you must either be dead already or in the forensic scientist community (coroner, law enforcement officer, and the like). There go all my hopes and dreams...

Are you an organ donor? How does it work?

I am. I would donate everything if I was a lifesaving (organ) candidate. You have to die on a respirator to be able to donate most organs. Medical professionals leave the ventilator on to keep the organs oxygenated, so you typically need to die in a hospital to be an actual lifesaving donor. If that were to happen to me, I would like every usable part of my body to be donated. I would not donate if I was only a life-enhancing (eye and tissue) candidate. To explain: if I were to die at a scene, instead of in a hospital, with no chance of my organs being used, I would skip donation all together. Often times, life-enhancing parts are not immediately used. The idea of pieces of me being put up on a shelf, reserved for future use just doesn't sit well. If you don't qualify to be a lifesaving donor, but opt to be a life-enhancing donor, your coroner will make arrangements with the organ/tissue bank once your body arrives at the morgue. Each place follows different procedures. Your body could be sent to the tissue bank or a procurement team may come to the morgue and collect what they need there.

Please keep in mind that what I have shared is my personal choice. Anything donated, even life-enhancing organs, can make a huge difference in a person's quality of life. Consider the options and your feelings about each of them. Make your decisions based on what you believe is best.

Is there a way to know how someone's organs were used and who they went to?

There are no guarantees. You could ask the coroner's office what agency did the harvesting. The agency likely wouldn't be able to tell you specifics, but they might be able to say something like, "Her long bone went to a person in Michigan who had bone cancer. They were able to resect the old area of bone to use so now this person is cancer free and can walk again." In circumstances where the donor family would like to have information about the recipient, the transplant agency will act as a liaison between the two parties. Let's say the recipient would like to know about the person who donated a particular organ. The recipient would contact the transplant agency and the liaison would contact the donor family and let them know that the recipient would be interested in making contact with them. If and when the donor family is ready, they'll use the liaison to respond and ultimately they'll be put in touch with each other.

I've heard medical professionals treat you differently if they know you're a donor, and they won't try as hard to save you if they know you're an organ donor. Is this true?

Not in my experience. The medical staff will do everything in their power to save your life. I have never heard of a doctor intentionally letting a person die so they could use their organs. There is absolutely no personal gain for them when you donate.

Should one decide to donate their body to science, does the family ever get the body back so they can bury or cremate them?

Unless otherwise specified, the body is cremated and returned to the family within two years. It's usually much quicker than two years, even just a few weeks, but the most I've ever known about was two years.

Does donating my body cost money?

No. But there are parts of the process that can cost money. Each company has their own process, timetable, and so forth. I actually just recently learned that there are research companies that will do non-transferrable donations, where they take all kinds of various tissues for research and then cremate the rest of the body and return the ashes to the family, all within 4-6 weeks. It's totally free to the family! They also work with regular donation foundations to do what are called shared donations. So, let's say you die, and you're a candidate for organ donation. Your transferable organs will be taken and then this company can come in, take what they want of your body for research, then cremate the remains and return them to the family. Again, all at no cost to you! Also, they have a guarantee program, so if you're alive but on hospice, let's say, and you sign up with them, they'll take your body and cremate you and return your ashes for free. Even if normally you'd be declined as a potential donor, or the agency doesn't have need for tissue at the time of your death. They will still provide your family with their services to include transportation of remains, filing paperwork, and cremation at no cost to you or your family. Not all candidates are accepted, but it's worth looking into if you're interested.

OTHER, LESS COMMON OPTIONS

In addition to these mainstream sorts of decisions, there are a few that are far less common (and, not surprisingly, much more expensive).

- Mummification: This is a very meticulous and expensive process of "eternal preservation." Summum, the only company in the U.S. that provides this service, can mummify you for $67,000. This process can take upwards of 90 days to complete and it's the only form of permanent preservation currently available. In addition to being mummified, you can have an art form casket (think gold-plated Egyptian-type caskets) specially formed and designed for you. Seriously, this has got to be the classiest way to go. It's recommended that your mummified body be kept in a mausoleum/ sanctuary to avoid extreme temperature changes. To learn more, visit www.summum.org.

- Cryonics: Deep-freezing human bodies to preserve them for future use. Now this one got me. I gawked at the Alcor Cryonics website for hours, reading all the FAQs and learning about the process. I have to say this is one of the coolest things I've heard of, as well as one of the most bizarre. (I'm currently imagining my entire family and I, heroically emerging out of the frost, hand-in-hand, 5,000 years after our deaths.) In order to really understand cryonics and a person's reasons for wanting to be artificially frozen, you have to evaluate the definition of death and when exactly death occurs. Many of us consider someone to be dead once their heart stops beating. Alcor, a company that preserves humans in extremely low temperatures, only considers someone to be dead if the brain has been severely destroyed in a way that no longer allows thoughts, memories, and other brain-related functions to be accessed. So, if your heart has stopped beating, but your brain hasn't experienced trauma, Alcor doesn't consider you to be dead. Although you will be declared legally dead, Alcor would come in (preferably within a few minutes of your heart stopping) and begin the process of preserving you.

The hope is that in the future, when our understanding and use of medical technology increases, you will be fully "revived" and can continue to live life after being "awakened." The concept is fascinating and there's a lot of research and science backing up Alcor's information.

As far as the cost, Alcor states, "Most people pay for cryonics with life insurance, and since the actual cost of that depends on your age and health, to find out your specific cost you would need to shop for life insurance. Alcor offers two options: for whole body preservation you would need a minimum policy of $200,000, and for neuropreservation you would need a minimum policy of $80,000...Other funding options are available besides life insurance, including trusts, annuities, and prepaid cash or equivalent. Alcor members also pay annual dues."[xiv] If you have some time and any amount of interest, check out their website, www.alcor.org, (I highly recommend the FAQ page!)

What happens when someone dies and the family has no one for a funeral and/or no way of getting the money together?

If a family just doesn't want anything to do with the person, they can essentially give up their "rights" to the person by signing a form allowing us to cremate. However, in doing so, they also give up all assets that the person has. Those assets then go to the county to be sold to help defer the costs of cremating/managing the death. Most of the time, when people hear that, they just go ahead and pay for a direct cremation and then sell the personal property themselves. However, it doesn't always happen that way. I have a lady right now who is unclaimed. She literally has nobody. We will get authorization from our state's attorney to cremate her and then hold her cremains here. I'm working with a volunteer agency that does ancestry searches to help coroners and medical examiner's offices locate next-of-kin for unclaimed bodies. Hopefully they'll be able to help locate someone who would like to claim her cremains.

What do you want to happen when you die?

I will be buried. We have our plots in the cemetery associated with our church. I want a wooden casket with champagne-colored velvet interior. I want to be wearing pajamas and a robe and to be covered with a blanket. I would like to be buried next to my husband (who will surely die before me!). I would love bagpipes at my funeral, but, I'm not sure I'm that important. People would be all, "Geez, she's dead and she's still pretentious." However, if I were to be cremated for some reason, I would want my ashes mixed with concrete and made into a statue. A statue that my family could have in their yard. I feel like that idea is sentimental, without being too creepy.

I still have no idea what I want to happen when I die! How do I make this sort of decision?

Honestly, you just think about it. Ask the people who will be around to remember you questions like, "Would you rather come to a cemetery, leave flowers and think about me or would you rather have my ashes and do something special with them?" You can come up with several thoughts and see what works for you and your family. This is a great conversation for parties!!

A NOTE FROM JACQUIE

Most of us will have some sort of traditional service through a funeral home. We'll have a visitation followed by burial or cremation. Or a direct burial or direct cremation without any visitation. Research some or just think about what your family traditionally has done. Ask yourself what you like and what you don't like about it. Talk about it. And if you could all just do me a solid, go ahead and write down all of your demographic information, doctor's names, family contact information, and wishes upon death. Just keep that in a file by your front door and mark it "For the Coroner." No one will even notice, promise. And if they do, there's your opening for a healthy discussion about death! You're welcome.

THE BODY FARM

IMAGINE WALKING around a field with patches of forest and random manmade structures scattered about, completely surrounded by a razor wire fence. While taking in the surroundings you freeze and divert your step to avoid crushing what appears to be the remains of a small child's arm or leg. The bones, dirty and worn, almost blend in to the soil. As you continue on, a distinct, yet almost familiar smell, like meat left out far too long, begins to saturate your nostrils. You make your way further down this manmade trail, passing cage-like contraptions containing skeletal remains scattered among shreds of flesh and clothing. Eventually you arrive at a mattress holding what appears to be a weathered, naked body. The smell sinks further into your nostrils as you observe the disfigured skin of what was once a living person. The sound of the swarms of flies buzzing in and out of the body's orifices echoes in your ears. Distant calls of vultures surround you as they wait for the area to clear to continue their pillage. Patches of deep purple skin, rotting under the glow of the hot sun, seem to be melting into slime right before your eyes. A mass of synchronized movements catches your gaze and you zero-in on a hoard of maggots, feasting on this bounty of flesh.

This is only a glimpse of the various scenes laid out at The Forensic Anthropology Center (FAC) at The University of Tennessee, more popularly known as The Body Farm.

If you're like me, you're probably a mixture of disturbed and intrigued right now at that mental imagery. Though the idea of human bodies being stripped naked and dumped out in nature, left to the animals and elements to desecrate, while researchers study the effects may seem horrific (or incredibly awesome depending on what level of messed-up you are), there are tangible benefits to this important research taking place.

Anthropologist Dr. William Bass opened the facility in 1987. Since then, the research done here has aided in the training of law enforcement officers and those involved in crime scenes as well as the education of hundreds of students and researchers. This place has had a direct hand in solving real-life crimes and significantly increased our knowledge of the decomposing body.

Since the establishment of the Forensic Anthropology Center, five additional, similar establishments have opened up at universities around the country. Various research projects are conducted by students and researchers in the forensic anthropology and other related fields with the aim of furthering our understanding of decomposition as well as improving methods and techniques of gathering this information. Depending on the specific goal of the research, corpses are placed in various conditions and left to decompose for a period of time. During this period observations are made and information is gathered, specific to the aim of research. Think of it like the science experiments you conducted in high school—with a few dead bodies added to the mix. Documenting every phase of decomposition to create a guidebook for law enforcement, observing the effects of insect presence during decomposition, and cadaver dog training make up only a few of the interesting projects happening at these Body Farms. Are you ready for the best part of it all? You can donate your own body to the cause!

So, let's say you decided to donate and your fresh corpse is ready for use at The Body Farm. What happens next? The FAC at the University of Tennessee will pick up your body, free of charge if it's within a 100-mile radius of them. Farther than that, arrangements need to have been made by you prior to death or by a family member. Upon receipt, your corpse will be placed at the Anthropology Research Facility (ARF) and assigned an identification number. They have the outdoor facility where the decomposition projects take place as well as a state of the art lab. Depending on the projects currently underway, your body will either be used as part of a decomposition or skeletal remains project. Regardless of the use, all corpses will decompose naturally. If you're chosen for a skeletal remains project, once you have fully decomposed, your remains will be cleaned and added to the Bass Donated Skeletal Collection. No matter what the use, you can rest assured that your body will serve to perpetuate the research and knowledge of body decomposition and play a role in the aid of solving real-life crimes.

Sounds pretty neat right? If you're sold on the idea entirely, the FAC recommends doing a few things: The first is to express to your family and even your physician your desire to be donated. Anyone who will be responsible for making decisions upon the time of your death needs to be made aware of your wishes. Noting it in your will is also important, but not completely reliable. Often times a will is read after the funeral and by that time it will be far too late. Can you imagine the horror of cremating your loved one only to discover their dying wish was to be donated? Talk about awkward. Don't do that to someone! Start looking into your options and discussing it now. After you've made a decision on where you'd like to be donated, set up a plan for how your body will get to the destination. Look into your state laws on transferring bodies and form a plan of action. Many places, like the University of Tennessee, have a form you can complete to register for body donation upon death. This is the final important step that needs to be completed to ensure your body ends up where you want it to go. By doing this you're alleviating your family of another taxing form to complete during the fresh wake of your absence.

THE DETAILS

NOW THAT YOU'VE had all this information thrown at you, it's time to start preparing and making some decisions. As someone who shows up on a scene with little to no knowledge of the deceased, I feel it's extremely important (and oh so helpful) to have some information written down, somewhere easily accessible, in the event of your death. Go ahead, grab a pen and paper and start writing some of this down!

The death certificate is the most critical document to be completed in the event of a person's death. Nothing can really be done with regards to life insurance, settling of estates, account transfers, etc. without the completed death certificate. To help both your family and those completing the death certificate, having the following information on-hand and up-to-date is a real life-saver (whoops, another bad pun!):

BASIC INFORMATION:

- Full Name (including maiden name or other names or aliases ever used)

- Current Address

- Date of Birth

- Social Security Number

- Mother's Full Name including Maiden Name

- Father's Full Name

- Marital Status (If spouse is female, include maiden name)

- Name of informant (person handling) for your death certificate information

- Veteran? Yes/No. If yes, you should have a copy of your DD-214 for a proper marker and whether or not you want full military honors (usually provided by local American Legion or VFW)

- Number of years of schooling

- Place of Birth (City, State or Country)

- Primary Occupation and Industry (even if you're retired) (*Example: Nurse/Healthcare, Laborer/Construction, Teacher/Education, Homemaker/Own Home*)

CRITICAL HISTORY:

- Primary Doctor (full name and location)

- Specialist Doctors (*Example: cardiologists, oncologists, etc.*)

- Most Recent Diagnoses (*e.g., high blood pressure, high cholesterol*)

- Current Medications (e.g., *lisinopril, simvastatin, aspirin*)

- Description and date of all surgical procedures (*e.g., appendix removed, 1965; triple heart bypass, 1998*)

FINAL DISPOSITION:

This is the last piece needed to complete the death certificate. What exactly do you want to happen with your body when you die? Be very clear and detailed with your requests. You should let your family know which funeral home you prefer. Decide on your final resting place and include instructions and information to make it all happen when the time comes. Some options to consider:

- Burial (name a cemetery)

- Cremation (note any particular desire to keep ashes, bury ashes, divide ashes, spread ashes, etc.)

- Entombment (include the name of facility, location, instructions, and other pertinent information)

- Full body donation/research (include name of recipient organization, location, and contact information)

- Organ Donation (List your wishes as well as other pertinent information)

You also have the option of going to the funeral home of your choice and pre-paying (at today's prices) for a funeral service. This enables you to prepare most of these details ahead of time and alleviate any financial burden from your family. It's called "Pre-Need Funeral Planning." I promise you, your local funeral home will be delighted to help you set it up, and your family will be so relieved to have those details taken care of. Regardless of prepaying for the service, you can start setting up some specific funeral-related details. Plan and document things like whether you would like a wood or metal casket, crepe or velvet casket interior, color of interior, open or closed casket service, flowers, church services, music choices, Bible readings or other religious readings, and of course, the very most important part: the funeral luncheon.

Another thing to consider is what you want to be buried in or laid out or waked in. My personal preference is for pajamas, a robe, socks and a blanket. But I know some of you prefer to spend eternity in your Sunday best. Whatever you want is totally appropriate. Also, in case you're wondering, you will need underwear and a bra (for women) on when buried. If not provided, the funeral home will use a pair of underwear from "the drawer." I promise you, you want your own! If you're completely outraged by the thought of being forced to spend all of eternity wearing underwear, a stranger's no less, you can specifically request to be buried without them. Just be sure it's noted in your final wishes.

You can also plan what you would want your obituary to say and what papers you would like it published in. You may not know exactly all of the particulars, but you can certainly create a template of things you'd like included. For example, I want my obituary to list how I die because I know people always wonder that. I don't want to leave anyone hanging. I want a very specific and well-written obituary. In fact, I've already decided that I want Korttany to write mine for me. (No pressure, right?) If you know someone you'd like to write yours when you die, go ahead and ask them sooner rather than later. Give them time to come up with some really good material so you can go out with a bang!

Keep in mind that everything listed here does not serve as your final will and testament, nor is it an official legal document. I encourage you to make an appointment with a lawyer today to prepare your will. You will feel as if a weight you never even knew you were carrying has been lifted once you have that completed. The information we're suggesting you have documented is purely to assist those involved in the aftermath of your passing. Bits and pieces of what you've written will coincide with what's in your official will. However, a last will and testament is commonly read days to weeks after the passing of someone, which will be much too late to make some decisions referenced here. Wills also often contain information that you may want to be kept private (inheritances, estate settlements, letters from the deceased, and special wishes) until after you've passed, thus keeping them from being readily accessible. The decisions we encourage you to make here *need* to be discussed prior to your passing and this document is the perfect conduit to ensuring the start of a healthy dialogue between you and your loved ones.

If you have all of that information written down along with your decisions for your final wishes, and have a last will and testament in place, then consider yourself officially prepared for death! It sounds a little morbid, I know, but the reality is that having these things in order now ensures that the burden placed on your family will be light during such a tragic time. Now, your final job is placing this information somewhere safe and relatively accessible (maybe even in a few places), and letting those close to you know where to find it in the event anything happens to you. Set calendar reminders to update the information every year or when something important changes. Use this opportunity to talk about these decisions and make sure your loved ones have all of theirs completed as well!

AFTERWORD

Well, we did it! Above all else, I hope this book has helped you make the important realization that death is normal. It doesn't have to be the uncomfortable, grim dialogue we constantly avoid and bury deep within ourselves. Let's get out there and talk about things like the fact that we want our cremains shot into the sky as a firework display, or that we want to be buried commando (who wants to spend eternity with a wedgie, anyways?), or that we'd like our body to be thrown in the woods and studied by anthropologists. By normalizing the conversation about death, we're allowing ourselves to prepare for this imminent event, helping those around us navigate handling the details when the time comes, and gaining an understanding of the thoughts and wishes of those we care about. So, please, take a few minutes to sort out your final wishes on paper. (Go ahead and save the money you were going to spend on a gift, like a Snickers bar, for your coroner. This document will be more than enough! Promise.) Then make it your mission to start the conversation, share your wishes and connect with those around you on a deeper level.

Have questions not answered in this book?

Visit Jacquie's website: www.askacoroner.com where you can submit your questions to her and learn more!

A FINAL NOTE FROM JACQUIE

I feel like I should just write the lyrics to Green Day's "*Good Riddance (time of your life)*" here. I feel like that song sums up so much of what this book is all about. Think about it: time grabs you by the wrist and directs you where to go. Death is going to happen. Time doesn't stop for anyone. It's extremely cliché and true all at once. Let go of your worries so you can enjoy your life and the lives of those around you. Precious moments don't belong on shelves. Try to create the types of memories your family will drag out to talk about at your funeral. Embrace opportunities to create these memories. Simple, everyday memories. You don't need an extravagant trip – you need an hour in your backyard with your kids, a small gathering of friends around the table swapping stories.

I see so much regret and so much fear of death, that people have forgotten how to live. However, I also think it's important to realize that the way we as a family or a community manage our deaths (funerals, visitations, etc.) is how we develop our culture. This is what we do. This is how we honor our dead. It's okay to talk about it, it's okay to bring our children to funerals and visitations, and it's okay to explain death in a manner that's age-appropriate. Also, and probably most importantly, hold your coroners accountable. We're here to help you navigate through a tragedy. We are your GPS in a completely uncharted territory. We can help you.

If nothing else, I hope you read this book and developed a better understanding of how the death industry works and some of the options available to you. I also hope it encourages conversations within your family about your own wishes for after you die, because when your time comes, your family will want nothing more than to honor you by granting your final wishes. Don't make it a guessing game. It's something unpredictable, but in the end is right...I hope you had the time of your life.

RESOURCES

BODY FARM:

- Colorado Mesa University, Forensic Anthropology Research Center: www.coloradomesa.edu/firs

- Southern Illinois University Department of Anthropology: http://cola.siu.edu/anthro/cfar

- Southeast Texas Applied Forensic Science Facility: www.shsu.edu/~stafs

- Texas State University, Forensic Anthropology Research Facility: www.txstate.edu/anthropology

- University of Tennessee, Department of Anthropology: http://web.utk.edu/fac

- Western Carolina Human Identification Laboratory: www.wcu.edu

CAR SAFETY:

- Child Safety Guidelines: www.safekids.org

- Distracted Driving: www.distraction.gov

CREMATION:

- Angel Flight Fireworks: www.angels-flight.net

- Bios Urn: https://urnabios.com

- Celestis, Space Missions: www.celestis.com

- Eternal Reefs: http://eternalreefs.com

- Life Gem Diamond Ashes: www.lifegem.com

CRYONICS:

- Alcor: www.alcor.org

DEATH INVESTIGATION:

- American Board of Medicolegal Death Investigators: www.abmdi.org

- Scientific Working Group for Medicolegal Death Investigation: http://swgmdi.org

DONATION:

- Body Donation: http://www.lifelegacy.org

- Organ Donation: https://organize.org

ENTOMBMENT:

- Mount Pleasant Group: www.mountpleasantgroup.com

GREEN BURIAL:

- http://www.sierraclub.org/sierra/2015-4-july-august/green-life/how-be-green-grave

IMPAIRED DRIVING:

- Facts & Statistics: www.cdc.gov/motorvehiclesafety/impaired_driving

MOTOR VEHICLE DEATHS:

- Highway Safety Research and Communications: www.iihs.org
- National Highway Traffic and Safety Administration: www.nhtsa.gov

MUMMIFICATION:

- Summum: www.summum.org/mummification

ORGAN & TISSUE DONATION:

- U.S. Government Information on Organ and Tissue Donation: www.organdonor.gov

SIDS:

- SUID and SIDS: www.cdc.gov/sids/aboutsuidandsids

SUICIDE PREVENTION:

- National Suicide Prevention Lifeline: www.suicidepreventionlifeline.org, Call: 1-800-273-TALK

SUNNY DAY SUICIDE:

- Direct Effect of Sunshine on Suicide: www.ncbi.nlm.nih.gov/pubmed/25208208

WILLS:

- Final communication service: http://www.ifidie.org/
- More information: http://www.alllaw.com/topics/wills_and_trusts

TO THOSE WHO HUNT BARGAINS

This book wouldn't be complete without giving a huge shout-out to those who made it possible! Without each and every one of your thoughtful questions and contributions to the thread that started it all, this book wouldn't be here today. Though primarily referred to as "Internet strangers" throughout our writing, you're truly a special and unique group of people who have changed our lives forever. The love, support, sarcasm and wit you provide is unlike anything we've ever encountered in "real-life." When faced with life's situations, we often find ourselves thinking things like, "What would Julie or Erms or PineRhine expect me to do? Maybe I need to follow Sunny's recommendation and call an attorney! I should just ask Kato or Supergirl for some sound advice." And, of course, we can't even pick up a make-up brush without thinking of Pashed. Each and every one of you has impacted us, and this book, in one way or another. Sincerely, we thank you.

And now, for the most important question of all: Do we get a badge for this?

ABOUT THE AUTHORS

KORTTANY FINN has always had a knack for writing stories. She spends a great deal of time sharing humorous anecdotes about daily life with her delightfully brainy husband Brendan and their three children: Prescott, whose tiny body can hardly contain the amount of wit and charm he possesses; Valerie, who has been both astute and determined since day one; and Adelle, who is simply just the sweetest. Korttany's love of sharing her own stories quickly expanded to those around her. She is devoted to taking other  people's experiences, tuning and polishing them to perfection, then bringing them to life in print. When not writing, Korttany mentors teenage moms at a support group that provides parenting tools and resources.

 **JACQUIE PURCELL** is married to John and has a plethora of kids. Her son Alex is fully grown and in the process of joining the US army. For many years it was just the two of them and it wasn't uncommon for Jacquie to arrive on scenes with little Alex in tow. Later in life she married John, who according to Jacquie, must possess loads of patience and blind love to be able to put up with her. Together they have three kids: Benedict, Molly and Josephine (who is affectionately referred to as Coco). She currently balances full-time work, full-time family and full-time campaigning. Her home is a hot mess of laundry, dishes and wall-to-wall playdough at any given moment in time, and although cliché, she wouldn't trade it for the world.

BIBLIOGRAPHY

[i] http://www.iihs.org/iihs/topics/t/general-statistics/fatalityfacts/overview-of-fatality-facts

[ii] http://www-nrd.nhtsa.dot.gov/Pubs/811059.PDF page 2

[iii] "Direct Effect of Sunshine on Suicide." *JAMA Psychiatry* 2014; 71(11):1231-1237. doi:10.1001/jamapsychiatry.2014.1198 Published online September 10, 2014

[iv] "Direct Effect of Sunshine on Suicide." *JAMA Psychiatry* 2014; 71(11):1231-1237. doi:10.1001/jamapsychiatry.2014.1198 Published online September 10, 2014.

[v] http://www.cdc.gov/sids/aboutsuidandsids.htm

[vi] Brenner, Erich (January 2014). "Human body preservation - old and new techniques". *Journal of Anatomy*: n/a–n/a. www.wikipedia.org/wiki/Embalming

[vii] Schultz, John J., Michael W. Warren, and John S. Krigbaum. "Analysis of human cremains: gross and chemical methods." *The Analysis of Burned Human Remains* 4 (2008): 76.

[viii] http://lifegem.com

[ix] https://urnabios.com/

[x] http://eternalreefs.com/

[xi] http://www.celestis.com

[xii] http://www.angels-flight.net

[xiii] http://www.mountpleasantgroup.com/pre-planning/cemetery/products/rights/crypts

[xiv] http://www.alcor.org/FAQs/faq01.html#cryonics